WHAT WOULD BEN STEIN DO?

WHAT WOULD BEN STEIN DO?

Applying the Insights of a
Modern-Day Pundit to Tackle the
Challenges of **Business** and **Life**

BEN STEIN

WILEY

John Wiley & Sons, Inc.

Published by John Wiley & Sons, Inc., Hoboken, New Jersey.
Published simultaneously in Canada.

For general information on our other products and services or for technical support, please contact our Customer Care Department within the United States at (800) 762-2974, outside the United States at (317) 572-3993 or fax (317) 572-4002.

Wiley publishes in a variety of print and electronic formats and by print-on-demand. Some material included with standard print versions of this book may not be included in e-books or in print-on-demand. If this book refers to media such as a CD or DVD that is not included in the version you purchased, you may download this material at http://booksupport.wiley.com. For more information about Wiley products, visit www.wiley.com.

Library of Congress Cataloging-in-Publication Data:

Printed in the United States of America
   Stein, Benjamin, 1944-
   What would Ben Stein do?: applying the insights of a modern-day pundit to tackle the challenges of business and life/Ben Stein.
     p. cm.
Includes index.
ISBN: 978-1-118-03817-8 (acid-free paper)
ISBN: 978-1-118-17352-7 (ebk)
ISBN: 978-1-118-17350-3 (ebk)
ISBN: 978-1-118-17351-0 (ebk)
  1. Life skills–Handbook, manuals, etc. 2. Conduct of life–Miscellanea. I. Title.
HQ2037.S73 2011
646.7–dc23   2011029293

10 9 8 7 6 5 4 3 2 1

Contents

1

Marriage
A Big, Big Deal

FOR MOST PEOPLE in a free society who decide to get married, the most important factors in their lives are who they marry and how the marriage works.

Life is difficult. Out there in the world of commerce or agriculture or law or medicine or bureaucracy or the military, the individual is merely a cog in the machine. Expected to produce so many widgets, attend so many meetings, file so many income tax returns that the way he feels, the kind of mood he's in, all of that is extremely secondary to what he (or she) produces. What his or her output is for the production of the almighty dollar or the almighty spreadsheet is what counts in the real world outside the home. This means that the outside world is cutting you down to size (as the song goes) a fair amount of time. It leaves you feeling like your life is a routine, like you're a number, a brick in the wall (to quote another song). You—as a person, as an individual–do not count for a lot.

Bear in mind, there are exceptions. Some workplaces make you feel good about yourself and care about you as a soulful human being. But as far as I have been able to tell, these kind of professional environments are in the minority. It is great if you can get into one of them, but it's not a standard part of the workday to make the worker feel good.

Shelter from the Storm . . . or Not

However, if your home is a warm, cozy place with a warm, cozy spouse, you have a fortress against the pressures, anger, and cold of the outside world. This is no small thing. If your home is built upon the rock of love and understanding and caring, you have a shelter from the storm. (Forgive me, but I cannot stop myself from paraphrasing songs. Popular music is a major part of my life.)

To be sure, and I don't want to kid you about this, as many, many homes are not warm, cozy places. Instead there are many homes that are Roach Motels of anger, sarcasm, an absence of love, and constant fear of explosions of rage. Still other homes are poisoned pools of estrangement and deviousness.

How do you make sure you have the kind of home that works as a fortress and a Sleep Number bed to keep you comfy all of the time, no matter how badly Mister or Missus Recession blows at the door? How do you make sure you have a home in which you feel protected, and not threatened or bored or mystified by what is going on in there? How do you build that happy home you want?

There Are Two Major Ways

1. Making the right decisions about who you marry.
2. Acting decently and lovingly as a spouse yourself.

These might sound simple. They are in fact incredibly difficult. Let's first take a closer look at making the right decision.

2

Character Is Your Most Important Product, and Work Is a Life or Death Matter

BASICALLY, CHOOSING A mate of good character is what it's all about in marriage, as in friendships. One immense part of this is that the man or woman in whom you are interested in must be solvent. This does not mean rich; however, it almost always means being employed. One of the most ready ways to discover if a man or woman (a single one, at that) is of good character is whether or not he or she is gainfully employed. If he or she is not employed—is not going off to work each day to earn a purposeful dollar—you generally do not want to marry him (or her). Now I know what you're thinking. You're thinking, "That surely does not apply in a bad recession, such as we are having right now—2011—as you are writing this, does it, Benjy?"

Yes, I am afraid it still applies. Of course we know that many fine men and women have been laid off and have lost their jobs through no fault of their own. I am well aware of that and my heart breaks for those people. My own dear grandfather was unemployed for many years during the Great Depression; yet he was a fine man. But that was a *Great Depression*—where there simply was no work to be found. And, as soon as there was any work at all to be had, even difficult work, below the status he had been used to, he took it. We are not in a *Great Depression* now, and I pray we never will be again. We are in a time when work is exceptionally hard to come by for many people in many areas—but there is still work and in many areas there are labor shortages. (Think any of the major oil and gas and non-ferrous metals extraction states. Think Washington, DC, and environs. Think of the major agricultural regions. Think anywhere the would-be worker is willing to look day and night for a job and take what's available.)

My experience—and I could be wrong—is that if a man or woman really throws himself into it, he or she will find a job, even if it's not the job of his or her dreams.

I keep thinking of my wife's manicurist, who came here from the Far East, could barely speak English, and soon had three jobs keeping her busy around the clock. I keep thinking of my daughter-in-law, an East Indian woman who came to Los Angeles from South Carolina and simply walked her feet raw looking for a job and found one.

3

Work = Character

IF A POTENTIAL mate cannot—or worse, does not *want* to find a job—then this shows, barring some unusual circumstance such as a disability, a potential character problem. I am sure there may be some places in America where even the most assiduous worker will have trouble finding work. But in such situations, the potential mate can move to more prosperous climes, find work, and then ask the potential mate to move. A recession is wickedly bad, but it just is not anywhere near as cruel as a Great Depression and to say it is, by way of an excuse for not working, is a bad sign.

I will say it again: Absent extremely exceptional circumstances, a grown man or woman should be working prior to marriage (and—in most cases—after marriage, as well).

The better potential mate also has been *continuously* employed. You do not want someone who bounces from job to job every few months. You want someone who makes at least a good faith effort to stay on the job and do his best to be productive and get along with his fellow colleagues. My experience—anecdotal as it might be—is that marriages that last are made up of men and women in jobs they have held for a long time.

This does not mean they have to have had the same job all of their lives; although, that is not a bad thing. My brother-in-law, a successful lawyer in New York City and all-around great guy, has been at the same job since he graduated from Harvard Law School in 1962—which makes close to 50 years as I write this—and he and my sister have been married 48 years. However, having the same position throughout one's entire life is not a strict requirement.

Many fine people have tried several different jobs before they found the one that suited them. Your humble scribe has had many, many, different jobs and still does to this day. But I stay at them for some time and generally make at least a little

11

something of myself in each one. I do not say this to brag; I am merely making a point—that steady work, in my experience, shows a character suited to a productive marriage more than unemployment or bouncing around within the job market, getting fired here, or quitting in a pout there.

4

Work Is Not the Same as Looking for Work

I KNOW I will get hate mail for this, but it's true and worth repeating: A man or woman who is chronically unemployed, who cannot keep a job, who cannot predictably bring home a check—that is someone often with character problems, who—as far as I have been able to tell in my limited circle of acquaintances, is a major risk in the marriage department.

Heirs and Getting Real

You may well ask, "Does this apply if the person in question is of means or leisure and does not need to work?"

My answer is definitely, "Yes."

Our country is a very rich one at this point in time. It is not at all rare to *not* need to work—even among young people. But the ones who do not work, or who pretend to work while actually doing nothing more than producing pipe dreams of great wealth, these are—in my experience—not men and women of good character. They are dilettantes and playgirls, and not really suited to face life's many challenges. Therefore they are not suited to face marriage's challenges.

If any of my rich, unemployed, pipe-dreaming friends reads this, please do not be angry at me. You can still be great pals and I am sure you are. But until you have shown the discipline necessary to work and to *stay* at work, you have not been forged in the furnace that produces men and women of strong enough personality to be married and stay married. Being married, staying married—these are real challenges. High-carbon steel character is required, and nothing demonstrates this more than steady employment.

The Exceptions That Test the Rule

Now, a few caveats. The need for employment does not apply after a certain age. If a hardworking person has reached his late fifties or sixties and no longer needs to work and say, decides to devote his time to golf and charity, he can still be a perfectly fine marriage partner, and probably will be, in fact. As long as a man or woman has shown that he or she can work, over a period of time (relative to his or her age), he or she can be counted on to have satisfied the *work* requirement.

There is another large exception in addition to the *I've paid my dues by being married to you for 30 years* exception: To be considered a good marriage partner, a man or woman need not have worked on a factory floor or in an office or a shop continuously for a long period. Yes, I know I said that consistent work is important. But not all work can be consistent, steady work. For example, some men are real artists—not phony, fraudulent artists, but actual artists who make a living at it. Maybe that's the person in your life. If a person has an honest job that pays the bills, that's fine. This is especially true, again, when the nature of the work is sporadic. I'm reiterating this because my wife reminded me that when we got married, she was a lawyer (steady job, or so it seemed) and I was a screenwriter, columnist, novelist, and author of novels, diaries, and tomes about finance. Mine was sporadic work (although I always had a lot of it and could not keep up with the backlog) and hers was steady work, but it worked out fine. More than fine.

I was used to hard work . . . and so was she. It is that custom—getting work done and being accustomed to discipline—that is the main point. And it all comes back to character—the touchstone. If it is the kind of work that shows character, it's good work. If it's the kind of work that shows either no character or its twin, bad character, that's something else entirely.

I Meant "Honest" Work

If, for example, you have a person in your life who is intelligent and hard working, but his work is selling people fraudulent investment products, that person probably is not good marriage material. Honesty and trustworthiness are character traits that one wants in a spouse. So don't be fooled; hard work by itself is not a sufficient marker for good character.

Carefree Student Days

Now, what about getting married young?

Here, I admit a bias. I got married when I was a law student and graduate student in economics. My wife was an undergraduate in college. My parents got married when they were graduate students. My son got married when he was a student.

All of the marriages have lasted, or did last, a long time. My parents' lasted for 60 years, until my mother died. My wife and I have been married since 1968. My son has been married about three years, which is a lot considering that he is 23.

Many of my closest friends from the whole range of my life got married when they were young, usually while in graduate school. Most of those marriages have lasted, although not all. The line I can draw about which marriages have succeeded and which marriages have not surrounds—once again—discipline. The men and women who were self-supporting, by means of work in school, are the ones whose marriages lasted. If these men and women had the work ethic to keep up their grades and also bring home the bacon, they usually were able to have the grit to stay married.

If a man and woman, even as students, can run a household while learning and earning, he or she probably has at least some discipline, and again, this discipline is what it's all about.

I will say that if a young couple is completely supported by their parents, this possibly works against their turning out to be great marriage partners. They are basically just children in a playpen of marriage unless at least one of them is earning money for school in some way—even if it's by part-time work.

So, now that we've assumed you have found a hardworking man or woman, in a reputable job, earning a decent living, not running afoul of the law, not in a job that would make you afraid to bring him or her home to mother. What next?

5

Personality, No Divas Wanted

IN TERMS OF what makes a marriage work, first comes great looks and a great body, then personality. JUST KIDDING!!! Actually, you do want to be attractive to your spouse. If you are not physically drawn to a potential man or woman when you first start courting, you will probably not find that person more attractive as he or gets older, fatter, and more wrinkled. So, yes, appearance definitely counts.

But, let's get back to personality. All kidding aside, personality is absolutely vital. For a marriage to work, it is vital beyond words that your potential spouse has a pleasing personality. (And that you do as well; we'll get to more of that in a moment.) Accept no substitutes. Do not allow someone in your life who is judgmental, who endlessly finds fault, or who loves to pick fights. And, if a person ever, and I mean EVER, compares you unfavorably to a past lover, politely gather up your clothes, explain that you are feeling ill, get dressed, and leave and never come back. Don't call. Don't answer the phone or text or e-mail. Just move on. Trust me.

Men and women who are good marriage material do not ever say you are *less than* —in any area. Not ever. Yes, of course they can bring up an old flame to tell a funny story or to illustrate a non-critical point, but never in such a way as to compare you unfavorably.

I don't ever want to hear that someone else bought my wife a more lavish gift. (And I don't think I will, since my wife had cheapskate boyfriends until she met me.)

And Also No Divas

You do not want a wife or a husband who throws fits. Although that makes for good drama, you don't want your life to be drama. You want your life to be calm. (We'll get to that later, too.) You want peace in the valley. Marriages that are peaceful last. Marriages that are wildly up and down wind up in family law court.

You cannot imagine how many evil, controlling spouses there are in this world. I have had close friends whose wives spent day after day, year after year, screaming at them and telling them what losers they were.

Let's just get it straight: If you have a boyfriend or girlfriend who judges you, who gets drunk or high and abuses you, who—again—compares you with other lovers unfavorably, get the heck out of there in a great hurry.

You may hear your lover say, "I'll change." DO NOT BELIEVE IT. Human beings do not change. Or, to put it another way, human beings change so rarely that one might just as well assume that they do not change at all. Let's see the viper turn into a Cocker Spaniel for 24 months and then we'll see what's what.

Again, do not, not, not trust the people who abuse you, mistreat you, or belittle you. Don't even try to change them, even though they swear they will change: Just walk away.

There Are Several Close Kin to This Advice:

1. Childhood Counts

    If your partner has undergone some traumatic, deeply wrenching events in his or her childhood or youth, those horrors will always, and I mean always, come out to bite you. Not maybe. Not sometimes. Always.

    Children from abusive backgrounds deserve a huge warm blanket of sympathy. But even so, they will show signs of distress, and those signs of distress may make for difficult living conditions.

2. Drugs and Alcohol Are Not Good Wedding Gifts

    If your lover has a drug or alcohol addiction, be extremely wary. In general, long-term use of drugs leads to personality changes for the worse.

Abusing drugs and alcohol diminishes the ability to maintain focus and ambition and discipline on the job or in the home. The job suffers and then goes away. The business suffers and then goes into bankruptcy. It all goes bye-bye when drugs and alcohol are in use on a chronic basis.

Just as a word to the wise, potential mates who are habituated to drugs, dependent on drugs, addicted to alcohol, or even whose parents are in that situation are poor prospects for marriage. They can be saved, and I have seen them saved, but the odds are long.

3. Family Ties That Choke

Parents can be a trap. It is incredibly difficult being married, especially at first. You suddenly have turned a good chunk of control over your life to someone other than yourself. As I often tell my wife, the essence of marriage is that you are in the car on the freeway and one of you thinks the car is too hot, and one thinks it's too cold. One wants to turn on the air conditioning. One wants to turn up the heat. What do you do? How do you compromise?

If you have parents mixing in their views of the temperature or how fast the car should go or what lane it should be in, that gets to be even more trouble. Many cars nowadays have different temperature controls for different sides of the car. But as far as I am aware, no car has been able to accommodate viewpoints of those not actually seated in the car.

This, again, presents a serious challenge. It is one thing to have all of the problems of acclimating yourself to a totally sovereign other individual. To suffer many others messing in your lives, with their view being that they know best, is maddening.

Alas, that is the basic condition of in-laws and parents (not to mention siblings and children by prior marriages). If you find yourself in love with a man or woman whose parents routinely and offensively interfere, you are possibly facing serious danger.

If your lover has parents who are emotionally supportive but who butt the heck out whenever anything serious is at issue, you have won the lottery.

4. Money and Love

"The love of money is the root of all evil," says the Bible. Very likely this is an exaggeration. There are many other sources of evil, especially envy and jealousy, but certainly money and the infinite complications around it are at the root of much of what kills marriages.

If you have a potential spouse who spends money she does not have, who gets herself head over heels into credit card debt, then unless you have a virtually infinite amount of money, you are going to have problems. If you have a boyfriend who gambles away his money and who habitually loses his paycheck, you will likewise be in jeopardy.

By the same token (or maybe it's by a different token), the boyfriend who is maniacally cheap and goes berserk at even the slightest extravagance is a killer as well. Different attitudes about money lead to conflicts, fights, anger, and loss.

The really big problem is that men and women have extremely deep-seated attitudes about money. It is very hard to convince anyone that his attitudes about the long green are mistaken once he is set in his ways.

Money, so I read, is one of the great marriage saboteurs, and it's best to have someone in your life who at least generally shares your views on this dismal subject. I will be the first to say it is not an easy task to find such a person; so with that said, just realize that you *must* have at least some basis of trust.

Money is so basic, so fundamental, and generates so much anxiety, that unless you can see the other person's point of view and adjust to it, there is no hope the marriage will last. Conflicting attitudes about money lead to literally life-ending anxiety in some cases.

Love Is the Boss . . . and the Gangster

Now with all of this said, and read thoughtfully by you, I know what you're thinking. You are thinking, "But what if I really, really, really love him (or her)? What if my love is so strong that it compels me to overlook all of these issues that you so cheerlessly bring up, like a cruel bookkeeper instead of Cupid?"

I am telling you all of these mistakes you might make, because I have made them all myself. I have fallen for women with mental problems. I have gotten involved with vicious, castrating, psycho women—and been hopelessly in love with them. I have been wounded in love, and I have been wounded in hatred.

I have seen every warning sign flashing, and I have driven over the cliff anyway.

So, I know how hard it is to take good advice. In my own life I have made every mistake a man can make in love.

But, and this is a big but, I am still alive and smiling because I did recognize that I had made a mistake and managed to pull myself together, clamber back up the cliff, crawl over broken glass and molten lava, and find myself in a happy, warm home again.

I did many, many, wrong acts and deeds and hurt myself and those close to me badly while in the throes of love. But I turned back and even turned myself into a far more productive and useful human being. I did this through getting great advice, through 12-step programs, and through finding a God who would save me from harmful, abusive relationships. (This is another chapter racing towards you.)

So while I do realize that my advice will most likely not stop you from falling in love and getting hurt, it might allow you to realize—once you start really and truly hurting—the reasons behind your hurt. It's not fate. It's not destiny. It's not inevitable or permanent. There are certain types of people who are liable to hurt you. If you read this, look over at the man or woman sleeping next to you, or sniffing glue next to you, and say, "Hey, no wonder this hurts so bad. This is just the situation Ben Stein warned me about. I think I'll get the heck out of here. Better late than never."

If this were only for the few who realize the inevitable poison in their life, then this chapter were well spent. Think of this verbiage from me as a map. You didn't consult it on the way in, but maybe now that you're totally lost, you will feel like consulting it on the way out.

6

Getting Along in Marriage Is Not Easy—It's a Job

BUT A SUPER-IMPORTANT job. Let me try to explain it to you by anecdote.

Many years ago, when my beloved father was living, he religiously read the columns I wrote in the form of a diary for the *American Spectator*. In that column, long ago, I had a satirical name for our son's elementary school. It was affectionately satirical, but definitely had a bit of mockery mixed into it.

One day my father asked me, "Is that school important to your son and to bringing him up?"

"Indeed, it is," I said.

"Then why aggravate them by making fun of them?" he asked, very sensibly. He was right, as he almost always was, and I immediately stopped poking fun at them. That school was the linchpin of our lives when our son was young, and there was indeed no reason to take a cheap shot at an entity that was so important to us . . . and doing such a good job for us.

You can look at your marriage partner the same way. That man or woman is the most important person in your life. The marriage—that place that is heaven if it's happy and hell if it's not—is the most crucial part of your life. If it works out well, you have a major leg up on every other part of your life. If it does not work out well—if you are miserable and tormented in your marriage no matter what else is going well—no matter how rich and famous you are, nothing is going to keep you happy.

In other words, it is worth investing a heck of a lot in keeping that marriage going and keeping it happy. It is worth more than getting drunk or hanging out with your pals or showing off to your spouse how tough you are. It is worth almost everything else in your life.

How Human Beings Work

But how do you make the marriage happy? Well, first of all, let's assume you are not married to any of the desperate and unpleasant characters we discussed in the preceding chapter. Let's assume you are married to a fairly normal man or woman. (That's a very big leap, to be sure, since my experience tells me there are not too many really "normal" and sane men and women out there. But let's assume there are at least a few . . . and that you are married to one of them.) How do you keep the marriage with that person fulfilling and happy?

Really, it's pretty simple. You *work* day and night to make that marriage partner happy. You act as if you are a candidate running for office and your marriage partner is the last vote you need to win. You act as if the husband or wife is the buyer of the order so big that once you close the sale, you will be on Easy Street for the rest of your life. You make sure that within the boundary lines of dignity, you make your spouse as happy as she or he needs to be. You treat her as a life-or-death matter, and him, too.

There is a famous line from the Buddha that a Buddhist friend from long ago used to tell me:

"There are three rules of life: Pay attention. Pay attention. Pay attention."

Pay a lot of attention to your spouse. Pay a lot of attention to your spouse. Pay a lot of attention to your spouse.

That means . . . you campaign all of the time for that person's affection as if the presidency of the universe depends on it.

Now I don't really mean *all of the time*. Obviously, if you're ill or just hit by a car, you can sulk and moan. If you just got laid off, you can be sad for awhile.

But most of the time, you want to be as complimentary, accommodating, forgiving, cheerful, and lavish with praise as you can possibly be.

That man or woman you are married to is not your slave; not your whipping post; not your child. Like any other human being, he or she responds better to praise than to criticism. Like any other human on the earth, he or she wants to be noticed, appreciated, loved, thanked, and treated with respect. This is what you do. You treat that person with respect and love and forgiveness and gratitude.

Now some readers might say, "Hey, Benjy, this woman is my wife. It's her job to deal with my moods and to put up with me if I'm surly to her." Another reader might say, "Hey, he's my husband. I don't have to coddle him. He signed up ' . . . for better or for worse . . . ' If I want to be nasty to him, I can. That's the way marriage works."

No, It Isn't. That's the Way Marriage Doesn't Work

You have to treat your partner with respect. That person whom you order around and then ignore has a soul and a personality and wants to be treated with total respect. People do not like to be badly handled, and when they are, they take it hard and relationships wither.

This is big stuff. Think of how respectfully you would behave toward your boss if you knew he or she was considering a big promotion for you. You would be act like that boss was the king of England. But your spouse is far more important to your well-being than your boss. Your spouse is vastly more vital to your long-term happiness than your boss will ever be. If you find that you criticize your wife for something you would laugh off with your office colleagues, you are making a mistake. If you find you are picking on your husband over something that you would find cute or engaging in a friend's spouse, you have to knock it off.

There are thousands, maybe tens of thousands of books about marriage. For my money, the very best book you can find on the subject of how to make your marriage work is *How to Win Friends and Influence People* by Dale Carnegie. In that book, Carnegie lays out a sure path to get people to like you and want to be your friends and do what you want them to do. The basic ideas are to be complimentary and accommodating, to never pick fights, and to do whatever is possible to make the other person happy and content.

This book, this hoary chestnut, really tells you more about how to make your spouse content, and thereby make your marriage happy, than any other book I have ever read.

Now that lurking, alert reader will say, "Hey, what's going on? Why do I have to be the one who accommodates? Why can't he/she be the one who does the accommodating? Why can't I be the prima donna?"

The answer is simple: In a marriage where one is the diva, neither will be happy. The diva will never be satisfied with her diva-ness and the servitor will never be happy with his drudgery. But in a marriage where each seeks to accommodate the other, both will be happy. In a marriage where the goal is not to get all you want but to be as helpful as you can be; helpfulness, an even temper, forgiveness, and good faith become the watchwords; and love glows and grows. This happens to be fact.

In a marriage where each partner can count on the other to work for the other's good, there is a warm, soft, cheery atmosphere. There is not the fighting, sharpening-of-knives attitude that makes for short tempers and short marriages.

"To get along," said a famous politician named Sam Rayburn, once Speaker of the House of Representatives, "you have to go along." That was how he worked as a successful Speaker of the House. That is how you can and must make your marriage work: Getting along with your spouse comes ahead of anything else.

A good, lively sense of humor is a key part of this scheme. In one of my many 12-step programs, we have a saying. "If you can't laugh at yourself, you're missing the funniest joke there is."

Laugh, Laugh, I Thought I Would Die

Likewise, in a marriage, try to laugh *with* your spouse. Try to see the humor in everything you say and do. If you can laugh at yourself, if you can chuckle at your own obsessive-compulsive demands to keep changing the thermostat of your marriage, you will go a long way toward making your marriage last. A marriage where both sides—where both partners—take each other terribly seriously is like a stiff but fragile reed. It will break in a strong wind.

But a willowy, supple sense of humor as the spine of a marriage will bend but not break.

A good way to evoke that sense of humor is to seek to imagine what you and your spouse are doing is on YouTube. Would you laugh at yourself or would you think that what you are doing is really incredibly momentous? Or imagine that it's 10 years later, and you're recalling this incident. Would you consider it life-or-death important?

Lonely Street

To follow this last little engine of thought for another moment, when you are considering how angry you are at your wife or husband, try to imagine that you are so angry that you allow that anger to break up your marriage. Then imagine that for the rest of your life, you come home to an empty home, for not just for a day or two, but forever.

Try to imagine a life without that person who knows you so well, who has known you most of your life, and who knows all of your jokes from 20 years earlier. Or, think of re-entering the dating scene! The point is that it's difficult to imagine the Herculean effort of finding a man or woman who accepts your problems and issues, your bad moods, your bad hair, your belly, or your shrew of a mother. That is why it's important to always remember just how much effort you have put into making your marriage work. Try to imagine, again, just how lonely you would be without this man or woman who has put up with so much of your nonsense—and at whom you are so angry, maybe just for a few minutes.

It is not fun to be lonely—and especially not to be middle-aged and lonely.

That means, again, do whatever you decently can to make the marriage work. Go beyond what is adequate. Go beyond what is standard. Be super spouse.

This kind of behavior, this super-spouse behavior, most definitely includes forgiveness on both sides. Inevitably, you will say things that are hurtful, or at least taken as hurtful. If those words offend your spouse, you must apologize. Words have power. If you have used them, even inadvertently, to hurt or harm, you must thoroughly apologize.

Actions have power. If you have acted so as to hurt your partner, say by drinking too much at a party and saying wounding things, you must apologize.

If you have in some way betrayed your spouse—say by wildly overspending when you were supposed to be on a budget, you must very emphatically apologize, promise not to do it again, and mean it.

But you must also accept the apologies of your marriage partner. You must forgive, at least for a good, long while. I know it's hard to forgive some acts and some words by your spouse. They can cut like a knife.

I have seen this up close and personal in a marriage (not mine). I have seen the most vicious behavior I could ever imagine aimed at a husband by a wife—the wife wasn't even drunk! With all my heart, I believe that if the husband in this interchange had killed the wife in this case, he would have been forgiven by a jury of his peers. That is how hateful and hurtful the words were.

Yet this woman learned the error of her ways. She apologized and stopped her cruelty. She became a far better wife. And by the end of this marriage, the couple was extremely devoted to each other: caring, laughing, and growing old together. They are now are buried next to each other.

Forgiveness is possibly the most powerful force for good in the universe. In any situation in which there is even a little bit of goodwill, forgiveness will work wonders.

Along with the kind of caring and diplomacy I am suggesting, you can and will get a stupefying, good result from forgiveness. Forgiveness helps the forgiver and the forgiven.

Try it. Try to make treating your spouse as the most important person in the world your most important job on a daily basis. Try making forgiveness your routine response to misconduct by your spouse—as long as there is a meaningful apology.

The Breaking Point—and There Is One

However, all of that said, it is sad but true that there are some marriages that cannot be saved. There are some men and women who cannot be reached by even the kindest, most considerate behavior. They are out there, and I am sorry to say they are not rare.

In today's world, where so many young men and women are brought up to believe the world revolves around them, where so many of us genuinely think we are some sort of Fuhrer whose will cannot be questioned, there are some difficult characters to whom you will find yourself married. My pal, Phil DeMuth, likes to remind me that at least 25 percent of all Americans have a diagnosable mental illness. (Other mental health professionals I have talked to think that is a low number.)

So, by all means act with respect, deference, accommodation, a sense of humor, and forgiveness. And do it for a long time. If human beings change at all, they change slowly. Agonizingly slowly.

But if your spouse resists, if your spouse considers your helpfulness weakness; continues to boss you around; shrieks at you even more—makes you wish you were not married to her or him any longer—you should not be married to that person.

My dear pal, Ona Murdoch Hamilton, a simply brilliant psychologist, says that the acid test of any relationship is whether the parties feel happy being with each other. If they do, they should stay together. If they hate their time together, if they truly loathe and resent every tick of the clock while they are with each other, they should not stay married.

Be Careful

Bear in mind, d-i-v-o-r-c-e is extremely expensive and painful. It tests the good humor of even the steadiest personality. The lawyers who handle it are often shockingly well paid. The rage that comes out when money and property have to be divided is phenomenal. The fury that comes out when the custody and care and provision for children are under judicial review is mind-boggling.

Police consider domestic disturbance cases the most dangerous situations, because the parties are in such a fury when they get to the point where the police are called.

Imagine the state of mind of the parties involved in a bitterly contested divorce case. Imagine their condition of mind and soul. Now, imagine that's you. Imagine being torn apart by lawyers who have a lifetime of training in how to make you feel upset and angry about your life. Imagine forensic accountants who go through every piece of paper about money and property that has ever been seen—even by you, let alone owned by you. The motive behind this is to impoverish you and make you miserable and desperate.

Try to think of what your days will be like when the person who knows you the best in the world can and will use every bit of that knowledge to hurt you.

Try to think of your kids being turned against you. Try to think of every bad thing you have ever done in your life, every questionable remark, everything, all used against you.

Then try to think of how you could possibly function in your job or practice or business with that kind of warfare going on in your head.

That's divorce. Not always. Not even most of the time. But enough of the time that it's a very real danger.

In other words, consider carefully before you get a divorce. You might want to go on a long vacation alone. You might want to try a trial separation. You might want to see a therapist. But you almost certainly will not want to rush into divorce.

That being said, sometimes you still have to get divorced. It is better to be poorer and more alone than to live with your own Gestapo, your spouse. It is sad that it works out like this, but it sometimes does.

If your marriage does come down to a divorce, do your best to keep your cool and be as charming and friendly to your spouse as possible. Remember, you might someday change your mind.

I offer my own very bad self as an example:

In 1968, I married my first wife, a beautiful woman who had just turned 21 the day before, a blushing junior at Vassar College. In 1972, because of good and sufficient reasons, we became separated. In 1974, we got divorced. After a series of romantic comedies and tragedies, it became clear to me by late 1975 that my first wife was the only girl for me.

I can still vividly recall a trip to New Haven, Connecticut, in late 1975, to Elm City, where we had lived when I was a law student and grad student in economics. I walked in front of the tiny apartment house where we had lived and played. I felt such acute sorrow that my wife and I were no longer together that I could scarcely breathe. I thought my heart would just stop beating with melancholy. (This was in front of 34 Lynwood Place, in case anyone at Yale is reading this.)

Little did I know that my former wifey was in Washington, DC, practicing law and thinking the same thing. In a few weeks we were dating again, and in September of 1977, we were married again and, with a few hitches, we have been married ever since. We both tried not to slam any doors, and that allowed the miracle of our getting back together.

I realize that ours is a rare story. I realize that this kind of fairy tale twist almost never happens. But whether it does or does not, you have nothing to lose by consistently acting as kindly and well as you can bear to do to your former spouse.

Just for an example of why you want to do this . . . while my wife and I were separated, I started work at The White House as a speechwriter for the late, great Richard M. Nixon. I needed a Top Secret security clearance to turn that temporary job into a permanent job. The FBI interviewed my wife, who spoke glowingly of me, as I always did of her. The FBI man doing the interview told my wife he had never heard of a former wife speaking as highly of her ex-husband as she did of me. That was a factor in my getting that security clearance. (Just exactly why I needed a security clearance when I never saw anything even remotely connected with national security is unclear.) And, of course, the tides of fate determined that my job—and Mr. Nixon's—would be extremely temporary.

In any event, you have nothing to lose by being as polite and friendly to your ex as possible, even when it's a true challenge to do so. And you have nothing to lose in keeping an open mind about whether you want to go back and seek to open that door once more, as my wife and I did.

So, what would Ben do about marriage? Take it seriously. Take it as the immense part of life that it is. But also take it, as my dear friend, Al Burton, told me long ago, "with one eye closed."

The Clock Is Ticking

And one final note: As I was writing this little tome, my wifey and I went out to dinner with a large party of mature men and women at a club near our home in Rancho Mirage, California.

The women in the party were mostly older than we were: In fact, they were in their eighties. All of them except one were widows. As the evening went on, the women started to reminisce about their late husbands and the good times they shared with their late husbands. Every single woman at the table who had lost her husband teared up—even if the husband had been gone for 10 years or more. When the evening broke up, the widows—all of whom lived at the club, within a short walk or ride from the clubhouse where we were eating— were noticeably reluctant to go home to their empty homes.

It was heartbreaking. It reminded me for the millionth time, for the billionth time, that every day, every hour, every minute, every heartbeat I have with my wife is precious. More than precious. Spectacularly precious.

We drove one of the widows back to her home at another club near our house. She talked about how lonely she was at home with her dog. When we pulled the car up to her home, she insisted on showing her dog to me. And while the dog was cute and faithful, the house looked big and lonely and empty without a husband waiting there for her.

I put this out there for you: If you possibly can, find a good spouse. Once you do, treat that spouse like gold. There are very few men and women out there who will be perfect mates for you, or even close to perfect. Once you find one who even approaches the mark, do everything you can to make sure you do not come back to an empty house. And weigh in your heart extreme gratitude for every second you have together.

Of course, if your husband or wife is horrible, that's a whole different story.

7

Tipping

Now you may think that it's a big change to go from talking about marriage and its importance to talking about tipping at hotels, clubs, and restaurants (not to mention airports, taxis, limos, and train stations).

But there is a close connection. A life well lived is in large measure a life in which other people like you. In every single portion of your life, from preschool to hospice, from kindergarten to college to conferences to IRS audits, you are better off if you deal with people who like you.

For one thing, it just feels better to be liked. There is a distinct, warm flush we get from being well liked that is entirely different from that cold, lonely, slightly sick feeling you get from being alone and lonely and disregarded. In high school, in many ways the apogee of human feeling and existence, you feel on top of the world if you are at the cool kids' table at the cafeteria, and plain awful if you cannot get a date for the Valentine's Day dance. (Do they even have Valentine's Day dances any longer?!)

In college, if you're well liked you get dates with the best-looking girls and boys (do they even have *dates* any longer?); you get bid for the best fraternities; you feel cool as you walk around the campus; and you, well, you get the point.

Now to be liked in most of these situations, (and we will have more about them later), you have to invest a fair amount of energy. Or, more likely, you were simply lucky enough to be born to the world of coolness by having a certain mixture of good looks and self-confidence.

But what if there were a way, in short- and medium-term situations, to be not just liked but well liked (to paraphrase Willie Loman) without having to be good looking or cool or self-confident or rich?

There is. It's called being a good tipper.

The men and women you encounter in your daily life will not by any means all expect a tip. Your parents don't expect a tip. (Although it wouldn't hurt to try leaving one and see if it helps.) Your spouse *supposedly* does not expect a tip. (But try leaving little gifts on frequent occasions, and see how it helps.)

But there will be many persons you encounter in the course of a day who do expect a tip, and if you are a big tipper, it will make your life one heck of a lot better. If you are a regular at a restaurant, don't just leave the minimum you can get away with. Leave the most you can afford, and see how much better your service is and how much bigger smiles you get the next time you visit. For those of you who travel a lot, you might have your regular taxi driver meet you at the airport, and you will bound out of his cab with a smile on your face if he's been well tipped and is happy (except in New York, where the taxi drivers hate all mankind).

Your bellman at the hotel, your maid, everyone who works for you when you travel . . . they all live by the tips they get. They need that money to live. If you give them a big tip, they will love you for it, and they will have a better day—and go out of their way in making sure you, too, have a better day.

You want a better table at a restaurant? The captain works for money. Consistently applied, better tips will put you in tables that make you happy.

There is almost no better way to spend money to improve your life than to give large tips for personal service.

I learned this first from my beloved pal, Al Burton. I went with him to Las Vegas about 40 years ago and was astonished at what good tables he got for top events like Frank Sinatra or Elvis Presley. His *secret?* A carefully handed $20 bill to the captain. It meant the difference between being seated behind a pillar or enjoying the show.

So here's the lesson. The leverage involved in paying modestly additional amounts to waiters, captains, bellmen, and bell women is fantastic. Their salaries are modest. But generally (with some exceptions) a tip goes straight to their bottom line. They will appreciate it and make your life better. They need the money badly, and they will show their gratitude, unless they're insane.

We have a saying in Hollywood: "Be nice to the people you meet on the way up. You'll meet them on the way down." It applies in spades to the people who want, need, and deserve a tip.

(And, yes, I give more for good service than for bad.)

8

Work Is a Gift from God

WRITERS LIVE IN the real world, as I keep saying. As I have been writing this book, I have had interactions with a number of my friends. One of them, Phil DeMuth, is a super-successful money manager, student of finance, psychologist, and all around great guy. He works like a madman all day and all night, producing super-good returns for his investors and highly detailed, granular works on theories of investment, sometimes written with yours truly as nominal coauthor, even though Phil does 99 percent of the work and maybe more.

Phil is making money. Phil is mentally and emotionally involved with the world. Phil is happy.

Then there is M. M. is a middle-aged, extremely intelligent woman who does not work at all except as a very part-time docent at a museum. An unpaid docent. She is supported mostly by a modestly well-to-do writer and commentator who has a soft spot in his heart for her. M. is, again, an intelligent and loveable woman but basically lives in her own world of insecurity and concern. If something happened to her benefactor, she would be in extremely dire financial straits. Her considerable talents are not engaged with the world, and she has little pride of accomplishment in the world of work.

She is extremely unhappy most of the time.

C. is a friend of considerable years standing in Los Angeles. At one time, he was a high pooh-bah in the music business and made a fine living. However, he never developed any knowledge or rapport with music after the 1980s. He cadges small music production jobs here and there. But he is usually unemployed. His income is virtually nil. His days are spent caring for his many cats. He is cut off from the music business that was his life.

He has fantasies about immense projects that will happen and will make him rich. He is going to create a label that will sell Michael Jackson's entire catalogue in China (a fantasy meant to illustrate his fantastic lack of contact with reality). Whatever he does, he will do it big, so that, as he puts it, "I'll go out in a blaze of glory." It is all blowing smoke, and he knows it.

He is miserable almost all of the time.

D. is a beautiful, statuesque woman who once was the girlfriend of an immense power in the Internet world. He arranged for her to have a startlingly well-paying job in Internet ad sales at one of the major Internet sites. When he left the company that employed her, she soon lost her job. She has had only sporadic work since then, possibly because she likes to get into arguments with the people who are her supervisors. She is a capable woman, with extreme knowledge of the Internet, but she has not been meaningfully employed for close to a decade. She still has savings and lives frugally. But she is lonely not going to an office. She feels alienated and discouraged. She has been offered lower-level jobs in the world of the web, but she wants something commensurate with the level of responsibility and power she had when she was at the company founded and led by her former boyfriend. She is not going to settle for anything less, at least not for anything a lot less.

She is unemployed and thoroughly unhappy.

Or, take my friend J. J. is a highly brainy, handsome fellow in his mid thirties. He has never had a real job. He has (like another fellow I just mentioned) fantasies of getting a series on television, when in real life, he cannot even afford a car.

When I tell him he absolutely must get a job, he always says he will look for one tomorrow. He never does, or at least he never finds one. He lives by cadging money from his parents and from that same writer/actor fellow I mentioned before.

Recently, as a single man, he sought to find a girlfriend on an Internet dating site. He is, as noted, a handsome devil, and found many young women eager to meet him. When they found he took the bus and had no money; not just a small amount of money—*no money*—and no job; he rarely got a second date.

J. is a charming, empathic fellow. But he's miserably unhappy and lives constantly in fear. In fact, as I write this, he has had a close brush with homelessness. He was saved by a donation from that same actor/writer we already talked about. He celebrated his salvation not by getting out and looking for a job, but by having a movie-watching marathon with a friend. After the movie-watching marathon, he is still terrified and desperate.

Possibly you are starting to get the picture here?

Just to dot the i's and cross the t's, let me mention a pal of very long standing, from school days. He and I have been corresponding for some time now about what life is about. He has been saying it's not about "selling out," not compromising his artistic integrity (he is a painter), and not doing work just because it might make money. No, he must stay true to a vision of himself as artist/martyr that will keep him unemployed and angry at all times.

He is lonely and sad much of the time. He asked my opinion.

"Remunerative work that allows you to support your family is a gift from God. It is literal salvation," I said to him.

He is an honest guy, so he very kindly wrote back, "Your insight is the wisest advice I have ever gotten, but is it too late now that I am 65?"

It is never too late. Work is a gift from God. I will say it until the day I die. (By the way, J. has gotten a job as I am editing this, and he is happy.)

Freud said that the only two abilities a human being must have to be successful are to work and to love. Without work, an adult is not a full man or woman.

Yes, the money is a big part of it. In the real world, whether it's China or Britain or the United States, money is a basic part of life. Without money, there is fear, even terror, and utter powerlessness. Without money, one is barely human. Without money—and I don't mean millions, but enough to be self-supporting and avoid terror—one might as well be a lost dog.

Money of your own keeps you from being a totally lost, helpless, beggar: a poor atom floating pitifully through space.

But the beauty of work is far more than the money part.

Work connects you with the universe, as Freud once again so wisely said. It makes you feel that you are *part of* the whole human race and that you have earned your right to be here on this planet. It makes you feel as if you have accomplished something meaningful.

Samuel Johnson, the greatest essayist in the English language, said that nothing is a surer cure for any infirmity of the mind or spirit than work.

The Lord God, Jehovah, said that in the sweat of a man's brow he would earn his bread. And how totally right these words are.

It does not have to be actual sweat, but hard work, not goofing off on the job, not taking the boss's money for a job not well done, not cheating; I'm talking about putting in a solid day's work. This is what gives sustenance to mind and body.

There is just a great feeling about doing a job and doing it well that nothing else can touch.

Maybe I might be permitted to tell a personal story to explain. In 1966, I was a first-year law student at Yale. I was misdiagnosed (to put it mildly) for a small problem by the Yale student clinic and put on some medications that turned me into a basket case: ataxia; deep fatigue; loss of concentration.

I fell behind in my work and dropped out for a year.

When I got home and stopped taking the meds, my health revived, but I felt anxious and severely depressed. I lolled around my parents' house all day feeling worried and sorry for myself. My parents were supporting me and I lacked for nothing, but I felt awful.

One day, my father suggested that I would feel better if I got a job. It was probably November or December of '66. I opened to the classified section of the *Washington Post* and immediately found a job as an *editor/writer* for a highly regarded Washington publisher called the Bureau of National Affairs.

It was snowing the day I started the job.

I filled out my employment forms and was assigned a battered, gray, metal desk in an office filled with men and women who smoked. I was sent over to the Department of Labor to a press conference to announce some statistics about unemployment. I got a press release, took a few notes, and then took a taxi back to my office. (It cost 30 cents plus a dime tip!)

Then, I sat at my ancient Royal manual typewriter and wrote about 800 words of the story. I used the exact same format I had been taught as the editor of my high school newspaper.

I handed it to my boss, a fine fellow named Dan Harbor. He read it and said he was very happy with it. I heaved a huge sigh of relief, and went into the men's room and literally sang with happiness.

Yes, that was how happy I felt back then, some 45 years ago, to be doing remunerative, appreciated work.

As soon as I got back from the men's room, I was sent off to the Department of Commerce for a story about trade data. I was on a cloud.

Work satisfies.

Yes, you can beg. Yes, you can scam. Yes, you can live off relatives or friends. But those offer no emotional or psychological satisfaction. Actual work, the harder the better, turns the trick.

As I reported a moment ago, work connects you with the whole world. The whole of humanity, as my pal, Phil DeMuth, says, is sort of a giant beehive. You can either be a part of the hive, a part of the immense brotherhood and sisterhood of man, or you can be apart, a sort of parasite.

Note that I have repeatedly said that the work should be remunerative. I believe that to be true.

But there are exceptions: Work done to care for one's family and loved ones is generally expected to be without pay. But it's incredibly important work nonetheless and offers commensurate satisfaction. The work that men and women do to care for their children is astoundingly difficult work and is almost always unpaid. In fact, it's really all unpaid. But it is as vital as any work on the planet and offers unmatched satisfaction.

Work done to care for ill or ailing relatives or friends is also almost always unpaid, but it's phenomenally challenging.

And phenomenally emotionally rewarding.

Likewise, work done for charity or other worthy causes is worthwhile and self-validating. It is a lot better if it's paid, but it's great work even if it's not paid. Caring for the poor; for sweet, innocent animals; for the ill; these are fine jobs. They do not need to be paid to create self-esteem . . . but it's a lot better if they are.

Just as a personal matter (since this is a personal book), I find that working to help our fellow human beings and fellow animals (and to protect our earthly environment) is just about as good as any other work there is.

My own hero and mentor, Richard M. Nixon, famously said that there was as much dignity in cleaning out the bedpans of the ill as there was in being chief executive of the government. This might have been a subconscious statement of his feelings about the worth of the presidency. But it also was a meaningful comment on how much virtue there is in working to care for the helpless or afflicted among us.

One of my best friends is the famous prosecutor and writer, Linda Fairstein. She was the chief sex crimes prosecutor for the island of Manhattan for many years. She was Deputy District Attorney of Manhattan under the legendary Robert Morgenthau for decades. She is the author of umpteen *New York Times* best-selling mystery/detective novels.

She appears on panels of famous and powerful and successful women all over the nation. All of this has helped to make her a famous, well-heeled, lovely woman.

But it is her unbelievably hard, devoted work caring for her family that makes her a great woman.

Again, this world is filled with men and women who do the work that allows civilization to go on. Caring for children is the work that is at least as important—if not more—as heading up Cisco or Amazon. However, for most of us, we must work to pay our bills. My point here is that work is vital for self-respect and self-approval.

Your humble servant belongs to a program that helps people with mental health issues. What I have observed over the decades in this program is that when a sick (mentally sick) person gets a steady job, he makes an immense step up the ladder of mental health.

Once that step is ascended, then some modicum of self-discipline, self-control, energy, and ambition come into play. Then comes some bit of planning.

But it all begins with work. If I am dwelling on work in this tome, it's because I believe work is an almost supernaturally powerful force for good. Freely chosen, freely entered into work—done with the utmost of devotion—that's as potent a step towards mental well-being as there can be.

9

The Need to Save Money
Is Life or Death

I KEEP SAYING it—and it's true. We writers and actors and economists do not live off on a desert island. We live in the world. We interact with other people. Sometimes these other people tell us heartrending tales.

For many years while I was doing *Win Ben Stein's Money*, I had as a colleague a woman now approaching middle age as a member of our production crew. She was and is a highly capable, pleasant woman, whose work product was spectacularly fine.

After *Win Ben Stein's Money* ended, she got a far better job on a much bigger show and worked on it successfully for eight jolly years. Again, her work product was well liked.

Then, with zero warning, she was fired for absolutely no cause in early 2011. WHAM! Right out of the blue. She was given six weeks' worth of severance pay and asked to leave.

She was extremely dismayed. *Terrified* might be a better way to put it. She had savings equal to about three months' expenditures. Hollywood production jobs are notoriously hard to get. Even someone as talented as she is would have trouble getting the kind of steady work she had on her most recent eight-year run.

The situation gets worse. She has an enormous dog. For the enjoyment of the dog, she bought a home she could barely afford even when fully employed. Now, facing possibly prolonged unemployment, she couldn't possibly afford the home. She considered downsizing to a rental, but it was difficult finding one that accepted pets. She loved that dog the way parents love their children. So she was literally left with no clue for what to do.

So here's the lesson. While my friend fell into some bad luck, the reality is that there is a country in which about half of the working families have savings of less than two months' expenditures, and never imagine that they might lose their source of income. That country is called the United States of America. This is a country of wonderfully kind and pleasant human beings. I marvel at how sunny they are as I crisscross the nation on my endless travels. But it is a country of many wildly imprudent, slobby people where money is concerned.

This is a country where, as a matter of course, men and women use the last of their savings to buy big-screen TVs or boats or trips to Buenos Aires, always in the *magical thinking* delusion that things will somehow work out right in the end—just as they do in movies.

The problem is that life is not the movies. Things very often do not work out right. This problem of things turning out badly is especially cruel when it comes to money. So much of this country is exposed to likely bad outcomes where money is concerned that it approaches crisis levels.

It is so important that you not let yourself be included in this vulnerable, exposed group, that it's impossible to over-state the seriousness of the matter. YOU MUST HAVE SAVINGS.

Maybe you don't need them if you are a Rockefeller and you are under 16 years old. But everyone else needs them.

10

There Are Few Guarantees

THE UNCERTAINTIES OF life are limitless. The certainties are limited indeed. In today's world, there are no more safety nets to fall back upon for most people. Yes, there is unemployment compensation if you lose your job, and welfare. But try to live on either of those. Try to live on government handouts with even the slightest comfort. Try to live on welfare, and tell your pals you're on welfare.

This is real life. It isn't a high school production of *Hair* or *Rent*. It's embarrassing to share with your pals that you are on the dole. Unless you are an old-line hippie, you won't like it.

Think about it another way. Let's assume you're employed. If you got laid off tomorrow, how long could you live without starving? How long could you pay for the mortgage and the taxes and insurance and food? How long could you do it? If it's for a period of weeks or months, not years or decades, you need to save more.

As I write this, we are in a shallow and tentative recovery from a serious recession. There are about 15 million unemployed. There are tens of millions more living from paycheck to paycheck. I used to be one of them when I first entered the labor force after school. But I was a federal civil servant. I had no fear of losing my job. For those in the private sector—or even in the state and local public sector right now—there is no job security at all. Labor is simply the most easily varied cost for an employer. Good for the employer, but for the employee, it is a horribly upsetting situation to lose a job and have no money to speak of.

How do you get out of it? You listen to the advice of a friend from Poland who has been in the United States for about 25 years and is financially secure from her skills as an educator. "I save 15 percent of my paycheck every two weeks," she told me. "That's 15 percent of gross. I make sure I save it before I even consider buying anything with it."

I asked her why she was so prudent when so many Americans I know are so careless. "Because I come from a culture that knows that things do not always miraculously come out with a fairy tale ending," she said. "I come from a country where the worst possible ending is often the one that happens. And my father is not living and my mother is aged, and I know I have no one else to rely on except myself. So I save, and then I know that I have taken care of myself. I just don't have any other choice."

I see this attitude in my stunningly beautiful 23-year-old daughter-in-law. She is of partly East Indian heritage, and has the legendary caution of those great people in her blood. She saves at least something every month. I keep telling her my wife and I will take care of her, but she is more sensible than to be anything but self-reliant. I am not insulted by her attitude. I love it.

That habit—of saving—is a simply great habit to get into when you are young. If you don't get into it, if you live on the edge and you get fired or get sick, you are in terrible, terrible trouble.

A Firebell in the Night

Just think about it: What do you do when you run out of money? What do you do if your expenses outrun your money? Where do you live? How do you feed your family and/or yourself? What do you do? To me, it is amazing that there aren't more suicides than there are among laid off people. It is amazing that so many Americans can sleep at all at night when I consider how close to the precipice they are.

Not only that, but when an American gets behind on her bills, she really gets hammered by the powers that be. If you pay off your credit card balances each month, you incur no interest charges. But if you get delinquent, the bank that issued the credit card has little mercy. They can, and do, raise the interest rate on your unpaid balance to punitive rates approaching very close to 30 percent. This is bound to keep anyone in a state of perpetual peonage. (How it is allowed under law is a mystery to me. There once were usury laws. I guess they don't exist any longer.) The penalties for financial imprudence are cruel on an arithmetic basis as well as on a psychological and emotional basis.

There is a fairly straightforward way to avoid these kinds of crises: have savings. It is just so basically vital there are no adequate words to express it.

Again, just think what your life would be like if money stopped coming in. JUST THINK ABOUT IT.

If you really get it in your head, you will do something about it.

In the meantime just bear in mind what Samuel Johnson said (later borrowed by Ben Franklin). In times of adversity, he said, the best friends to have are ". . . an old wife, an old dog, and ready money. . . ." Make sure you have at least the third.

11

Your Beloved Parents

IF YOU ARE like most people, you appreciate your mom and dad just enough not to cause brutal fights at Thanksgiving. Yes, you might resent them for not buying you a car when you turned 16. Yes, you might begrudge them not praising your sixth-grade art project enough. Certainly, they were not the perfect parents you deserved. But you hold your nose and tell your parents you appreciate them.

Wake the heck up, and show really strong, glowing praise for your parents. It is an unbelievable amount of work to be a parent. It is as though, once you become a parent, you become a permanent indentured servant to the child. This is a non-stop job, and in short, is a hard gig. Appreciate it.

Your parents have often thrown away their independence, their good times, their money, and their chance to make their dreams come true to take care of you. You absolutely have to show in a clear, convincing way that you are deeply grateful. To begrudge them this kind of appreciation is just plain wrong and even immoral.

Plus it makes no sense. Your parents are—for most of us—the only people we can truly count on to take care of us in adversity. We must be as loyal and appreciative to them as we would be to a really good friend—because in fact, they are our best friends. To show love and gratitude to these people, to this man and woman, is just basic decency as well as basic good planning.

I often think of my own situation. As unscientific as it is, we humans tend to generalize from the microscopic sample of ourselves. So, since I am a human, I will do that, too.

I grew up with a huge amount of anger towards my mother. She was in many ways a terrifying creature. I don't think I ever met anyone as angry as she was in my whole life. I didn't like it. She made me fearful and nutty, and that condition would be my life sentence—or so I thought.

But as I grew older, and as I learned to pray for her instead of feeling anger towards her, the whole situation changed. For one thing, I realized that there were many other mothers who were also extremely angry. In fact, compared with some I heard about from pals in 12-step programs, mine was calm.

I tried to consider life from my mother's perspective. Unlike me, she had not been born into material comfort. She grew up in the Great Depression, and had fears of financial insecurity that I could only imagine. When she screamed at me because she didn't think I was working hard enough in school, she was only displaying the anxiety she had that only those with top grades could get jobs.

It was only when I started to think about life from her perspective that I began to truly forgive her and even to appreciate her.

With an attitude of forgiveness and gratitude, I was able to not only get past my anger, but to reassure her and help her feel better about herself. I especially made it my practice to listen to her stories about her childhood, repeated ad infinitum, for as long as she cared to tell them to me. Towards the end of her life, she told me that she never in her life dreamed that anyone could care as much about her childhood plight as I did, and that gave her as much happiness as anything a child could bestow.

And in return, I could find endless new gifts she had given to me that I could thank her for.

12

Does Death Really Come as the End? Maybe Not

NOW, WE MUST confront a dismal truth. I have mentioned many persons who are important in your life, especially your parents and your spouse. The cruel truth part is that in the likely course of events, your parents will die before you do. And there is a chance that your spouse will predecease you.

When this death comes, it comes like being hit by a truck. It leaves you speechless and gasping like a fish tossed up on dry land. It leaves you shuddering and in terror and loneliness.

There are, for most of us, two basic parts of your life: before your parents die and after your parents die. Worse by far, there is also a staggering division in the latter part: before your spouse dies and after your spouse dies.

The good part is before your parents die. That's the part where you're young, and you have someone to take care of you and to share your griefs and your sorrows. The bad part comes when, no matter what your age, you are an orphan.

It is just plain miserable to lose your parents. For those of us who have lost our parents, this sounds as obvious as a cinder block to the head. But for those whose parents are still alive, they might have a hard time grasping it.

I have not had the horror of having a spouse die, and I have had only one spouse, so I will just say that from what I have seen of losing your husband or wife, it's just about the worst thing in life.

But it's been almost 15 years now since my dear mother died—totally unexpectedly and suddenly—and almost 12 years since my beloved father passed away, with my sister and me holding his hands and reading him the Psalms as his dear, brave, old heart simply gave out. And in that time, I have learned something about how to cope with loss within the family.

I am now going to share with you the best of what I have seen about how to deal with the death of a loved one.

When my mother died, I was visited by one of the absolutely most intelligent, compassionate women on this earth, Dr. Barbara Bernstein, MD. Barbara, no stranger to loss, made this poetic point, which I paraphrase: "When your mother dies," she said, "it's as if someone put up a brick wall in front of your front door. That brick wall will always be there. It is not going away. But after a while, ivy grows on the wall. And after a longer while, roses grow on the wall. Then, while the wall is still there, it has certain loveliness about it. This is how the memory of your mother's good deeds changes the pain of her passing."

Barbara's analogy is well worth recalling when someone you love dies. You think the grief will be there forever—and in some form, it will be.

But it gets overtaken and covered up by the loving recollections of your loved one.

If you spend as much time as you can thinking of the good that your loved, dear departed did, you shorten the grieving period and lengthen the loving period.

When my mother died, on April 21, 1997, my father, who had never looked at another woman, was inconsolable. He was grief-stricken, alone, and miserable. My sister and I visited him frequently, but he was still desperately unhappy.

He took to writing my late mother a short- to medium-sized letter each and every day on his computer about how much he missed her and how he had spent his day. Obviously, he didn't e-mail them to her (she never learned how to use a computer—or even type—plus she was deceased). But he believed she could read them. And whether she could read them or not, he felt as if he were communicating with her. That made him feel much less alone.

When he went to sleep at night—or tried to—in the tiny double bed that he and my mother had shared since 1937, he often could not drift away. He took to listening to Mozart and Beethoven on his headphones, and that made an immense difference to him as well.

What saved him from utterly unbearable loneliness and endless misery though was friends. Not terribly long after my mother's death, a close friend since the 1950s, George P. Shultz, an incredibly capable and important former Secretary of Commerce, Labor, Treasury and State, under Nixon, Ford, and Reagan—then head of a mammoth construction company called Bechtel—invited my father to his wedding in San Francisco.

My father was so happy to be invited to this event, so happy to be back with his marching comrades from the Nixon, Ford, and Reagan days, he was literally lifted up. He was happy—well, not exactly happy, but uplifted—for the first moment since my mother died. George Shultz has been a spectacularly good friend of our whole family.

Then, not long after the Shultz nuptials, my father was called to the funeral of a dear friend in Washington, DC, whom he had worked with on foreign policy issues. At the reception after the funeral, the widow of the decedent told my father that she had tickets to the entire concert and opera series at the Kennedy Center, and perhaps he would like to take her to some of the events.

My father was in ecstasy. Literally in ecstasy. He was going to have not just company, but good company—beautiful, intelligent, caring female company for the first time since my mother died. He was a changed man.

I do not claim that my father was Moses or Freud. But he was a super intelligent man coping with a devastating loss. His idea of writing letters to my mother was simply inspired. Because he had known her for most of her life and his, he could automatically know how she would have responded had she been in a position to respond right away. In that way, he was really having a two-way conversation with her.

In my own little life, I have often used the same device when I am upset or fearful. I go to a quiet place, and I compose in my head a letter to my parents telling them what

I have been up to. I can well imagine their response—my mother's would be different from my father's—and in that way, I take myself out of the situation I am in at the moment and get some perspective on it.

Try it. You might like it.

13

Friendship Is Golden

BUT THE KEY word—by far, in this narrative—is *friends*. Because my father had toiled in the same vineyard for decades, because he had been a seer and pundit in Washington, DC, since the late 1930s, and a well-known one since the 1960s, he was the lucky possessor of a network of friends. He had few close friends—after my mother's death, my sister and I were by far his closest friends—but he had many fairly close friends and a wealth of colleagues.

His ability to draw upon that network of friends—to go to lectures, discussions, TV shows, seminars, meet and talk to old colleagues . . . often from before the war—that was miraculous for him.

He had been a scholar at the glorious American Enterprise Institute since 1974, and he had a treasury of friends and colleagues there. At the AEI there was even a separate dining table set aside for the elderly economists who dined there quietly and discussed monetary policy. (The waiters waggishly called them *The Wild Bunch*.) When my mother was gone, he had them as continuity and companionship. He also had the kind support—emotionally and intellectually—of Chris DeMuth, longtime head of the AEI, and one of nature's noblemen, just like my dear friend, his brother, Phil DeMuth.

When you are married, you may or may not need friends. When your spouse dies, you need them. Very fortunately, he had them.

He also had work—that great gift. His work was always in his brain and with books. So he could commune with that material and keep himself occupied. But I believe that was of far less importance to him than his friends.

Stock up on friends when you don't need them. If the day comes when you need them and you don't have them, you are in deep trouble. They are, as far as I can tell, the number one antidote to widowhood or widowerhood.

14

Don't Be Late!

As I KEEP saying, I don't live in an ivory tower, or in any kind of tower. I live in reality: In that reality events take place that scream to be topics in this book.

A few days ago, as I am writing this in the early days of March 2011, I had a call from a woman in late middle age who wanted my help getting her stories published. They were good stories, about her struggles adjusting to life in the United States after many years as a call girl in Buenos Aires under the thumb of a truly violent and oppressive pimp, or call girl maestro, or whatever he should be called.

I had met this woman at LAX, our giant airport here in LA. She had appeared to be a pleasant, sensitive, intuitive woman. I chalked this up to her *training*. I had met her for lunch one day in Beverly Hills. She was precisely on time and had behaved respectfully and even charmingly.

So, against my better judgment, I agreed to have her come out to my home in Rancho Mirage and bring 20 pages of her autobiography (that should have been a dead giveaway). I put aside extremely pressing work and met her, or thought I was going to meet her, at 2:30 in the afternoon. The time came, and there was no sign of her. When 2:45 came, there was still no sign. Then at 3:00 PM, just as I was about to put on my headphones and go to sleep for the hour, there was the sound of a speeding car slamming on its brakes right in front of my house. Then a car door opening and closing, and then a knocking on my door. There stood Evita, as I will call her, looking at me with a crazed grin. As she strode into my house, she exhaled. She reeked of gin. REEKED.

I told her I was a bit annoyed, and she asked why. "Because you're very late, and you arrived smelling of booze," I said.

"I'm only 10 minutes late, and I stopped to have lunch and a glass of wine with an old friend," she said. "If you don't want me here, I'll leave."

I didn't say anything, and she didn't leave, alas.

In the next hour, she told me she had, in fact, not had lunch but had drunk a couple of martinis, which, she said, was nothing for her, and she had no trouble at all *handling it*. She gave me her book excerpt to read. It was not badly written, but had so many graphic oddities that I felt embarrassed reading it in front of her.

While I read it at my dining table, Evita asked me if she might rummage in the refrigerator for something to eat. I told her to do so. I heard a great deal of noise, and after a few minutes I went into the kitchen. Evita had virtually emptied my refrigerator and put the contents in two large trash bags.

"What on earth are you doing?" I asked her.

"I am cleaning out the food that has passed its *use by* date," she said proudly. "I am protecting your health. Look at all this yogurt. It's at least a couple of months past its *use by* date. Do you know what could happen to you if you ate that?"

I did not mention the inconsistency of a woman who has been a call girl for most of her adult life, presumably engaging in all sorts of risky behavior with all sorts of risky people, with her fastidious approach to food's *use by* or *sell by* dates. I just sort of stopped talking to her except to say I would give her book a careful read after she left. She asked if I had any gin. Alas for her and me, Evita was invited to leave very soon after that. I didn't go to the trouble of putting the food back in the refrigerator, because I did not want to retrieve it from the trash barrel.

But I did mentally (and out loud) say a prayer of thanks to God for sending Evita my way. She helped me in many ways.

First, she reminded me to write a chapter of this book about how much I HATE, HATE, HATE it when people are late. I am a busy guy. I am a very busy guy and often a very tired, old guy. If I make an appointment to spend time with someone and am not getting paid for it, I expect the minimum courtesy of that person's being prompt. (If I am being well paid for my time, I could not care less if the payee is late.)

Taking up my time and making me cool my heels while waiting for a man or woman to show up so I can do him or her a favor is simply insanity. It is insane of me to put up with it, and it's insane of them to do it.

It is crossing a boundary I do not want crossed: the boundary of stealing my time. The boundary of respect. It's crossing too darned many boundaries.

To Be Late for Appointments Where You Are Not Paying People for Their Time Is Theft

Your humble servant knows a great many people who also occasionally make appointments with other people to do them favors. NONE OF US LIKES IT WHEN THE FAVOR SEEKERS ARE LATE.

It is insulting. It starts the meeting off on the totally wrong foot. It tells way too much about the tardy person, none of it good. It speaks of selfishness, carelessness, contempt, and an inability to follow through on commitments.

I am not sure I have ever had a truly good meeting with anyone who was more than a few minutes late. I am very sure that I have never had a good meeting with anyone who was half an hour late.

I make it a practice to avoid people who are chronically late—and so does everyone else I know in a position of even modest responsibility. (This doesn't even get to the parts about the food or the gin. . .)

So, if the words of this author mean a thing to you (and I don't blame you if they don't), take my word for it. DO NOT BE LATE.

15

Do Not Cross Other People's Borders without Being Invited In

THEN THERE IS the little matter of showing up drunk. In case you haven't figured it out by now, I do not drink . . . one day at a time . . . and do not like being around people who do drink unless they can handle it, without the slightest blink. My brother-in-law, Melvin, is such a person. He does not show it at all when he has a drink, and so I am happy to be around him when he has a modest drink. My pal, Joel, doesn't show it at all when he drinks either. So I don't mind his having a glass of wine.

But most people drink for effect, or so I have found. They don't drink for the taste or the smell. They drink to dull their consciousness. Guess what? It works!

Alcohol does dull consciousness. In some cases that makes people more fun and amusing to be around.

But by and large, when people drink they change, and not for the better. They become more aggressive, louder, more demanding, more irresponsible. The adult behavior monitors in the brain are shut down when people drink. This is just a fact—and again, it's WHY people drink.

If you feel you must drink, don't come to my home and empty my refrigerator. Don't come to anyone's home and empty his/her refrigerator.

Other people have their borderlines—on their property, their personality, and their beliefs. You do not want to cross them and run the risk of having your manuscript unread and your literary hopes dashed.

And in the same vein, when you show up at a person's home for any reason, do not presume that you are anything more than a guest. Don't criticize the homeowner's art. Don't criticize the owner's books. Just sit or stand quietly, and don't act as an art appraiser or judge of what is going on at the home in question.

Years ago, I was out at dinner with one of my smartest friends, Aram Bakshian, an extremely distinguished writer and public servant for many years, including as a speechwriter for Richard Nixon—where I was privileged to work next to him. He was also chief speechwriter for Ronald Reagan. He writes astonishingly fine reviews for many high-end publications, but he called me to task in a funny, but acute way, for doing just what I am doing now.

Aram and I, along with my wife and my pal, Russ Ferguson, were having Vietnamese food in Georgetown, and I was praising their bons mots. Then we paused to study our menus. Aram rather smartly said, "Well, now that we've all got our grades, we can order . . . ."

He was totally right, of course. Overdoing it with praise is fine with me, but with most people, or with some people, it is a form of sitting in judgment on such people. It used to be considered a sign of poor manners to even comment on the furnishings in a man's home. One man should not presume to discuss another man's *things* as my old pal, Frank O'Connell, said. That, too, is a form of boundary crossing.

The title of this book, to remind you, is *What Would Ben Do?*, and in this capacity, there are two parallel lines of response. First, what would I do with chronic boundary crossers? The simple answer: Unless they are members of the family whom I am bound to see and be around, I avoid them. If they want to empty my refrigerator, I stay away. If they want to show up late, I stay away. If they want to tell me how unhealthy I am, I stay away. I just stay away.

Second, I try not to cross other people's boundaries. I comment enthusiastically on politics or economics on TV or in print. But I do not tell people how to decorate their homes or what should be in their refrigerators. (I once did tell a hostess her pretzels were stale, and I have regretted it bitterly and ashamedly for years.) Even so, I am a born critic, and I probably do it without realizing how much I do it. For this, I apologize both for the past and the future.

Men and women must have borders in order to live, and I want to have mine and you want to have yours, and we only want them to be crossed by appointment.

If you have not made an appointment, don't cross.

16

I Am Just Like You, Only I Am Me

LIKE YOU, I sometimes awaken in despair and filled with suicidal thoughts. Well, maybe that's not like you, only it is like me.

Usually, this happens when one of two things is happening: Either I am coming down with a cold and/or flu, or the stock market is tanking. Actually, let's be honest. It could also be just because I have not gotten enough sleep. I am a maniac for sufficient sleep—as you should be—and if I don't get enough, I am in a bad, bad place.

I have been to enough meetings in which people have been talking about their moods to know that many of my fellow humans get up in the same mood. Despair and thoughts of gloom and doom are part of the general mood inventory for us humans.

Nevertheless, they hurt like the dickens. It actually is painful to awaken feeling that way. It is almost like awakening and having a headache or a stomachache—and I have had plenty of those, too.

The pain—psychic and physical—doesn't just have to come when you awake. It can come after a tiring day of work. It can come after a tiring and frustrating day of shopping. It can come at any old time, and when it does, it hurts.

In fact, I have sometimes found myself looking for ways to eternity after a day of just doing a lick of work and then thinking about absent friends and missing them and longing for them. I actually find myself contemplating suicide more often than is even remotely sensible.

However, in my long life, I have found ways to defeat these feelings, and I am now going to share them with you, my kind readers.

First, if you can, go back to sleep. There is nothing, absolutely nothing on this earth more restorative than sleep. The human body and brain need sleep. I do not know how sleep works, but somehow when you are unconscious, it's as if a major repair shop in your brain opens up. Microscopic repairmen go to work and start fixing whatever was wrong, and suddenly, you feel one heck of a lot better.

My late father's late professor, the genius free marketeer, Frank Knight, used to tell his students, "Never waste any time you could spend sleeping." When my Pop told me that, many years ago, I thought it was a joke.

But how right the brilliant Professor Knight was! There is nothing—not sex, not drugs (well, maybe some sex and some drugs) that makes you feel as good as sleep. "Sleep, that knits up the raveled sleave of care," as Shakespeare wrote.

Sleep puts the pieces of the jigsaw puzzle of your brain and your personality into the correct picture. You ignore your body's desperate need for sleep at your peril.

Those among us who claim they can get by with minimal amounts of sleep are just plain lying. They think they are getting by on five or six hours, but they are not. They are really sleep deprived and they would be doing their whole selves a big favor by adding a few more hours to their night's sleep.

(In particular, I observe certain failings or failures of judgment in the behavior of those who think they are getting by on just a few hours of sleep. If I may say so, I particularly observe failures of moral judgment on the part of those who think they are getting by on a small amount of sleep.)

But some of us cannot just go back to sleep. We have work to do. So what do we do when we awaken feeling down or when that feeling hits us in any part of the day?

Here I refer you to the single most important saying I have ever heard about the human personality. Long years ago (my favorite phrase) I was at a 12-step meeting. I was feeling despair about my career. A middle-aged woman with a sweet face said to me and the group, "Well, I feel really bad this morning, but I have learned that feelings come, and feelings go, and feelings are not facts."

Feelings Come, and Feelings Go, and Feelings Are Not Facts!

If I say this over and over again, it is because it's vital.

However you feel at any given moment . . . it's going to change soon. It will change as you rest. It will change as you eat. It will change as you get some work done.

Get it into your head: Feelings come, and feelings go. My experience is that even when I have felt the absolutely lowest I have ever felt in my life, those feelings come and go. A good meal, a compliment, passing by a lovely landscape feature, a joke, a feeling that I have accomplished a little something, getting some solid work done (see above), all of these events can and will change your mood.

I find that exercise in particular changes my mood. So does being in water. "Rock me on the water," said the gifted songster, Jackson Browne. He was referring to sex on a waterbed, but he was right about the water part. If I can drag myself out of bed and swim for a little while, I feel enormously better than I did before.

But the point is not really exactly what I do to change my mood. The point is that if I know my mood is going to change, I will not feel as if I am permanently locked into that down mood.

Then I will not feel suicidal. I hate blood tests. I hate and fear needles of any kind. But if I know that the needle will only be in there for a short time, I can laugh my way through it . . . usually.

Just so with despairing moods. If you know they will not last long, you can get through them.

I am not a physician. There may be some people whose sad, despairing moods are so long lasting and painful that they cannot see any light at the end of the tunnel. I do not pretend to be an expert in that situation. I do know that the people in my 12-step meetings almost always can see that their bad moods will not last forever and can therefore get through them without medication.

Listmania

I also find it very helpful to make lists of good things.

My first list is usually about what I am grateful for: living in and having been born in America. Having loving, supportive parents; having a great sister; having a super-fantastic wife; having a sweet, handsome son and a sweet, almost unimaginably beautiful daughter-in-law; having my dogs; having a swimming pool; never having been seriously ill so far—although it will happen for sure; having great friends like Phil DeMuth, Barron Thomas, Russ Ferguson, John Coyne, Aram Bakshian, Tim Farmer, Bob Noah, and above all, Al and Sally Burton; and many, infinitely more gifts, all of these go on my list, and by the time I have done this for a few minutes, I am almost always feeling a lot better.

This insight, offered to me for free by a woman who I had never met before, has changed my life permanently.

Feelings come, and feelings go. This is well worth remembering.

17

You Are Not at the Center of the Universe

ANOTHER THOUGHT THAT helps you get through despair was offered to me by my lifelong dear friend, Arthur M. Best.

Arthur, who is smart on a cosmic scale, told me that the way he beats the blues is to take a look at what's happening to him, and then to say, "So what?"

For example: I find my life savings have been negatively impacted by a stock market correction. "So what?" It will come back, or I will die before I need it, or I will make adjustments in my lifestyle.

Another example: I awaken with a sore throat, a particularly nasty ailment. "So what?" Hundreds of millions are also awakening with sore throats today. How big a deal can it be?

Then, closely related, there is the Hydrogen Bomb of mood improvers. I know this is a staple of my life, but I offer it to you, my faithful readers: When in despair, just think, "I am one of seven or eight billion people on this planet. I am not Superman. I am not Spiderman. I am just another mere mortal. Nothing that happens to me is terribly important."

This is immensely freeing. To know that I am not the center of the universe, that I am just one of billions—that really takes the pressure off.

Then there is another mega-monster of self-helping your mood. I also learned this at a 12-step meeting: I am here. God put me here. Whatever flaws I have—and they are plentiful—this is how God made me, and I will be fine just being the flawed human being God made me.

I do not have to be perfect. I do not have to wake up every morning feeling like a comic-book superhero. I am just an ordinary human being, and that is spectacularly freeing. Why . . . it's almost as if my mother said to me, "Benjy, you don't have to get grades as good as Jeffrey Burt's or Carol Brimberg's or Stanley Sitnick's or Jerry Akman's. You are just fine the way you are."

That's how powerful this incantation is.

If you can actually learn that the solution to much of life is to accept yourself, and not hate yourself and find disgusting maggots in yourself to loathe, you can escape despair most of the time.

18

The Next Indicated Action

SOME MORNINGS, I used to wake up (what do I mean, *used to wake up?* I still wake up!) thinking, "What can I do today to redeem myself and to be as big and powerful and important as I can? What can I do to permanently reboot my life so that no one I know is as important and rich and powerful as I am?" Or, I might just think, "How will I figure out what the hell I am doing here on this planet?" Or, I might think, "What can I do so that I can outwit the stock market?"

If I am smart about my life, I won't have many mornings like that from now on. In fact, I stopped having many mornings like that some years ago when I had a certain epiphany coming from a man at the fabulous 12-step meeting I used to attend regularly in Malibu. (This meeting was perhaps the best use of my time that I have ever experienced.)

The suggestion, coming straight from a famous book, was that I should just think about what I wanted to have for lunch that day instead of wanting to redeem my life and change the world—and then to DO THE NEXT INDICATED ACTION. That might be filing or writing a few pages of a book, or whatever small chore was in front of me.

This seems like surrender, but in fact it is more than a surrender—it is an acceptance of reality—and it makes no sense to fight reality. Maybe if you are Colonel Gaddafi or Benito Mussolini or Saddam Hussein you can defy reality for a time. But most of us cannot. We had better stop trying to do superhuman tasks, and just do what's in front of us. That might sound like the formula for a small life.

In fact, it is the formula for a sane, happy, calm life. And no life is happier than a calm life. No life is happier than a truly peaceful life.

Eat

Then again, there is the small matter of nutrition. I don't mean here trying to do some nutritional wonderwork that will allow you to live to 125. I mean just getting some food into you at sensible, regular hours through the day.

It is amazing to me how many people think they are doing themselves a big favor by starving themselves. They are not. They are throwing their whole lives and bodies off balance by not feeding their bodies and brains.

19

You Are What You Drive

I LOVE CARS. I love driving my cars (unless I am stuck in traf-fic). I feel as if my cars are my friends. I can count on them. They are like totally reliable friends and family. In a way, my cars are the most reliable, trustworthy part *of* my family. I can be sure they will do what I want, when I want, unless they are broken. They won't have a bad attitude. They won't sulk. They won't get drunk or high. They will protect me. I just get in the car and suddenly, I am about a thousand times as powerful and smart and better looking than I was a few sec-onds before. It is like magic, only it's real.

I Love My Cars

Now, you may say, "Wait a minute. They are just steel and glass. How can you feel so good about them?" Because they make me feel so good about myself, that's why. They make me feel as if I am a God. On my feet, I am just an overweight, old man who walks around at about the speed of other 66-year-old men. But in my car, I am lightning fast. In real life, I am overweight. But in my car, I am in perfect shape. In my real life persona, I am often tired and feel defeated. In my car, with a full tank of gasoline, I can do anything and go anywhere. When I am having a bad morning, as I often do (because as much as I sleep—10 hours or so—it's never enough), when I get into my car and turn the key and the beast roars to life, I feel like a whole new person.

I know I said it already, but think about it: Your car is never tired and never depressed. It is never angry at you for something you did or didn't do. It doesn't feel as if you owe it anything. It is just there to carry you around—more than that—to transform you from a pitiful peon of a mortal into an immortal knight in shining armor. Plus it says a lot about you. Maybe that's not the way it should be, but it's the way it is.

What your car is, how prestigious it is, how sophisticated you feel behind the wheel: These all become part of who you are. You are identified to valets and other drivers and people you meet in large part by what you drive. You tend to be identified even to yourself by what you drive. You manifest yourself to the world as a winner or a loser very largely by what you drive. Again, this should not be the way it is. We should all be judged by our faith and by our works. We should be judged by what is in our souls. But in real life, we are judged by what we own, in large measure, and this includes what we drive.

A few days ago I had to take my wife to rent a car, because hers was damaged. She rented a little Toyota instead of the mighty Lexus (itself a Toyota) she normally drives. "I don't feel like me," she said after an hour. She didn't mean she felt better. She meant she felt worse.

Many moons ago, I was a screenwriter and producer, pitching ideas and story lines and scripts at the studios that dominate the motion picture business. I had a problem with my car, and I needed to get a new one. I asked my dear pal, Barron, what kind of car he would recommend. Very wisely, he said, "Whatever car makes you feel confident and powerful and sure of yourself when you drive through the studio gates to pitch a script or have a story meeting." He was totally right. Many a time I arrived at a studio to try to sell a story line. Of course, I was basically just a beggar there to sell pots and pans. But because I had arrived in a Porsche 928, I felt as if I were someone of note—a winner—not " . . . a schmuck with an Underwood. . . . " as Harry Cohen, former head of Columbia Pictures, once called Hollywood writers. (Underwood was a major brand of typewriters long ago.) I could stand up to the studio buyers long enough to often make the sale.

A Car as a Mirror

It isn't a real mirror. It's a mirror of yourself as you want to be. The car companies spend billions advertising their cars as the cars of champions and cool guys. They create an image around their cars. Then you, dear friend, can wrap that image around yourself for a few hundred dollars a month. It is almost as if the car makers had spent all of those billions advertising you!

Of course, don't be insane about it. Don't buy more car than you can afford. Don't torment yourself with monthly payments beyond what is comfortable for you. But within the zone of financial comfort, get the car that looks the coolest.

Let's get down and dirty and honest here: We all want to be the cool kids in high school. That is our real goal in life. The easiest, fastest way to do it, for most of us, is to get a cool car. For pennies more than an ordinary, non-cool car would cost, you can get a car that makes you feel hip, slick, and cool. Try it. You'll like it. Again, prudence comes first. At some point, someone will probably collide with you. You should know that the laws of physics say that the car with the heavier weight transfers the velocity of the collision to the smaller car. So you want to be in the heavier car. And good sense tells you that you need great brakes and seat belts and airbags and all that safety equipment. But I will tell you something else. Life is really short. You don't have that much time to be cool. It is sensible to use the time you have to be cool. It just feels better.

The Hell Machine

I know I have talked about this car issue quite a lot. But the book is about what I am interested in, not what some environmentalist who could not care less about cars thinks is important. So, I will tell you this final car story.

In 1972, I was in terrible pain and had been ill for quite some time. I had a difficult job that I was not well suited for—namely, as a trial lawyer for the Federal Trade Commission, working on an extremely challenging case about the advertising for a fruit-flavored drink called Hi-C. It was not a great case, and it should not have ever been brought. But it was brought, and I was in charge of it. I had two of the smartest people on the planet working with me on it: my lifelong pal, Arthur Best, now a distinguished law professor in Denver, and Gale Miller, now a judge of the Colorado Court of Appeals. But it was still not a good case, and I felt sick much of the time I was working on it.

One day, the inspiration hit me that I should have a truly cool car, and that would make me feel better. I earned a pittance, but everything was fantastically less expensive in those days. Somehow, and I really do not remember how, I found a red 1962 Corvette for sale in a small town in Virginia. (Probably by now it's a very big town.) It cost $1,750. (Yes, $1,750. That's not a misprint.)

As we drove through rural Virginia to get it, Arthur kept calling me, "Benjy Jo," and it made me laugh every time. I picked up the car from some young mechanic who had made a few mistakes customizing the car (like putting the brake fluid line right next to the engine manifold, which soon created a hole in the brake line and made me have a small accident). But otherwise it was the car of my dreams.

I drove it back to DC at about 120 miles per hour and loved it for a long time. ("Corvette, me love you long time.") Then I took it to the "Film and Revolution" class I taught part time at American University, probably the best job I have ever had. The female students loved it. There was amazing ooh-ing and ahh-ing over it. There was a lot of romance connected with that car—and with my being " . . . so young, thin, and hip . . . ," as my student, Marla Bane, told me years later.

In that car, that cost me all of $1,750, I felt like James Dean. I felt like Elvis. I just felt amazingly cool and slick and self confident. I felt as if I were who I had always wanted to be.

My mother hated that car. It made a hugely loud, rumbling, throaty roar. She called it the hell machine.

The Corvette felt as if it wanted to eat the other cars on the road. I once caught rubber as we say, shifting from third to fourth at 100 miles per hour on the Dulles Airport Access Highway. That is, the car had so much torque power that it burned rubber going into a new gear at 100 miles per hour.

I FELT LIKE A DEMIGOD IN THAT CAR, and I believe it got me back to sanity and halfway decent health after the devastating blows of practicing trial law. That is what a car can do.

I still have a photo of me in that car, with long hair and a mustache, and no fat, and when I contemplate my current, aging, gray, fat self, and look at that photo, I still feel great.

Cars are life changers. This is superficial, but it's also deep and deeply superficial. You ignore their power at the peril of missing something big. Arthur Best is still my dear friend, and almost 40 years later, we still chuckle at " . . . the night of Benjy Jo. . . . "

20

The Absolutely Fastest, Surest
Way to Get Rich Quick

PART OF MY time, I live in Beverly Hills. It is a lovely neighborhood, with trees and stately homes and many Bentleys. It also has fine outdoor restaurants and crazy, old men who stop to ask me questions as I eat my spaghetti and meatballs.

One of the men routinely asks me, "How can I make a million dollars really fast?"

I always tell him I have no idea, but that in no way stops him from asking me the same question the next time I see him. As I wander around the nation from airport to airport, other people come to me and ask me where to invest their retirement savings. I always tell them I cannot offer any guarantees, but a judicious mixture of about 70 percent in a wide-ranging index fund, say, the Vanguard Total Market Index Fund, or the VTI, and about 30 percent in a fund of short-term US Treasury instruments, say the SHY, should do quite nicely. I wish that had been my investment posture all of my life. I did have some spectacular winners, like Berkshire Hathaway, but I also had many spectacular losers. I would have done better with just the broad index fund and a short-term safe leavening of Treasuries.

Truth to tell, however, my pal, Phil DeMuth, and I have written so much about this that I don't think I will belabor the point right now.

The more important news I have to tell you is that if that crazy man in Beverly Hills had asked me how to get rich quick, I could have given him a useful answer.

The state of being rich is primarily a state of mind. It really cannot be addressed by mere arithmetic. I can say I am rich if I have $20 million, but then someone can come along and say I am poor if I don't have $100 million, and, boom, I might feel poor. I can think I am rich if I have a home with a swimming pool under the stars, but if someone comes along and tells me he has a yacht that has a bigger swimming pool

than I have on dry land, and he can swim on any ocean anywhere on the earth any time he wishes, I might be tempted to
feel poor.

However, if I genuinely feel that I am content with what I
have, I am rich. The absolutely surest way to feel rich is to be
happy and satisfied with what you have right now.

This cannot be taken away from you if you don't let it be.
If you can banish envy from your life (a big *if*), and can genuinely concentrate on what you have and not on what you
don't have, you will be rich.

I swim in a pool with many people who are arithmetically
high net worth people. Very few of them seem to me to feel
satisfied. Very few of them seem to me to be truly content.
But then I have some friends in Sandpoint, Idaho, who have
little in the way of material goods but are content with their
lives—and to me, these people are genuinely rich.

One of my two or three favorite restaurants on this earth
is the Bottle Bay Resort. It isn't a resort like the elegant hotels
in Aspen or Montecito. It is just a dock, a restaurant mostly
out on a deck, and a few extremely modest rooms above the
restaurant.

Many summers ago, I went there every day with my son;
his pal, Alex; and his father, my dear late friend, Peter Feier-
abend. On many days, I saw a handsome man in middle age
with a beautiful wife also in what I would guess to be her middle thirties. They positively glowed with happiness. Like the
fool I am, I assumed they were an heir and heiress. Otherwise,
why would they look so happy?

But I learned after a bit of investigation that they were
in fact the owner of a small, local automotive supply store
and his wife. They were not rich at all in material terms.
They just took a lot of time out of their weeks to spend
with each other, and because the husband owned his shop,
he could close it at lunch to spend time on the perfect Bottle Bay of Lake Pendoreille with his lady love. To me, they
were genuinely rich.

I have seen the billionaires at work and at play. I have seen their mansions and their yachts and their airplanes. Some look happy. But most look deeply worried, as if they were looking over their shoulders to see who was catching up with them.

I have gone over my stock statements and my comparisons of what I paid for my real estate with what I owe on it (ugh). Rarely did these make me feel rich.

But last night, after a fine sushi dinner with my wife; after a long nap with my precious dog, Brigid, lying on my chest, with her big, heavy, old head right in front of my nose; I got up and swam in my pool out here in Rancho Mirage, where I am writing this. It was about midnight. The moon was about half full. It was rising above a trio of tall palm trees. The moon painted the palm fronds a silvery blue. All around it were glittering stars, planets, and satellites. A jetliner taking off from LAX made a glowing contrail nimbus across the moon, and then another one came by, and then another . . . like strings on a stellar, nocturnal guitar.

The water was warm, and the moonlight shone off its miniature wavelets.

I thought, "At this moment; not my pal, Warren Buffett; not John Paulson, the spectacularly successful speculator; not anyone on this earth feels as good as I do. I am HAPPY."

At that moment, I realized—as I have many times—that to be happy is to be rich. It does not work the other way around. To be arithmetically rich is not to be happy. But to be happy—to be content with what you have—that makes you instantly rich. There is no tax on it (yet). There is no way anyone can steal it from you unless you cooperate, and if you are in the right frame of mind, it works every time. Real wealth is for those who want it.

21

Silence Is Golden

Now for a little silent interlude. Almost silent.

I travel constantly. CONSTANTLY. And what I notice, among other things, is that when you board the plane, and when you are waiting to exit the plane, the airline plays loud music over the PA system. For no reason. When travelers are already frazzled and frustrated and getting shoved around like cattle in a cattle car, they have to listen to psychological warfare music.

Why? Why do we need this noise? I also notice that when I am at a fast-food restaurant, which I am a lot, they're usually playing some darned music, and usually something I hate. If I am at a so-called fine dining café, which generally means bad service and food that's not as good as Waffle House but is 10 times more expensive, I get really loud, horrible music that kills my gargantuan appetite.

If I am walking in a shopping mall, as I often am, there is loud music being piped in. Rarely is it anything I like or can even bear. If I am in a dentist's waiting room, there's horrible music being played.

Why? Where does the idea come from that we need to have music beamed at us all of the time we are out in the world? Someone invented something called Muzak many decades ago, and it was to play music in elevators so passengers would not feel claustrophobic. Now that idea has become a monster, and it's killing our peace of mind. Music plays everywhere, making me feel claustrophobic and as if I were having mind control brainwashing beamed at me. I am being punished for shopping or getting my teeth cleaned or whatever I am doing.

Look, if I am going to hear music, I want to choose what music I hear. I don't want some stranger with completely different tastes from mine picking what goes in my ears and into my brain.

Better yet, I would like some quiet. The world is a frantic, busy place. The value in a world like that is peace of mind, not of getting jacked up listening to strange music.

I love this country. I love my daily life. I love it a lot. But I don't need loud, wacko music assaulting me everywhere I go. I would like some silence. It offers peace of mind: that invaluable treasure.

22

Gratitude, Revisited

As I wrote this, I got a call from a friend whose son is at a super-expensive for-profit *art school* that really exists to transfer money from the taxpayers to the owners of the school, as federally-guaranteed student loans make up most of the tuition. (The tuition, at a for-profit school whose classes are largely online, is as much as at Yale. This is made possible, again, by the sucker taxpayers and their betrayers in government.)

The friend, a middle-aged woman, complained bitterly that her daughter, the student at the *art school*, never thanked her or expressed gratitude. The mother was so upset at this that she was contemplating suicide.

I listened sympathetically and then hung up.

But as I did, I thought about how rarely we thank our parents.

I especially thought about how inadequately and poorly I thank my Father in heaven, who has made all of what I have possible. He made it possible that I get to live in this country. He made my successful, supportive parents real. He gave me whatever small talents I have. He gave me the health necessary to employ those talents.

We parents complain about the lack of gratitude our children show to us, but how much gratitude do we show to the Author of all the happiness we possess?

That is a major omission which we can and should rectify immediately.

23

A Day to Remember

As I KEEP telling you, I live in THE REAL WORLD, or at least in a very small, very privileged part of THE REAL WORLD. As such, events keep intruding into my consciousness that direct what I will write about today. I could write about anything, but what happens to me influences me greatly.

A few days ago I worked on a commercial for the Internet for a company that sells investment research. The studio where we worked was way out in Glendale, a long ride from my home. The people on the set were an interesting mixture, and texts, phone calls, and e-mails kept flooding in to my Verizon Voyager. From these, I respectfully ask to submit a few for your approval . . . along with the lessons I hope to have learned from them . . . and from the people on the set.

First, a view from the set on nose rings.

One of the men who was manhandling props and stage equipment was a likeable, intelligent-looking fellow with sensitive features. I would normally have trusted him to do anything for me. The only problem was that he had a huge, terrifying-looking nose piercing right in the middle of his nostril openings.

That, by itself, gave him a forbidding air. It was as if his nose piercing were saying, "Hey. I'm BAAAD. Stay away from me. I pierced myself just so you would know that if you come near me, I'll pierce you, too. I am so mentally unwell that I would do something you would not like. I would shock your bourgeois world."

Human beings have only one chance to make a first impression. With that nose piercing, he made a first impression that was bloodcurdling.

Why? I assume that he had some deep, psychological motive for looking the way he did. Many Americans nowadays have facial piercings. To me, they all look terrifying and as if

131

something truly horrible happened to them in their youth to make them want to torment their flesh by piercing it in such a public way. Maybe I am wrong about this. Perhaps men and women with piercings are the salt of the earth and the kindest, nicest people on the planet. Maybe they are smarter than I am, more capable than I am, or more trustworthy than I am.

But they sure don't look that way. They look as if they are saying, once again, "Stay away, or I'll hurt you!"

I would respectfully suggest to the people considering piercings that they give prayerful thought to just what kind of impression piercings make. Do they really want to warn people away from them? In a world where employment is often scarce, where men and women often go by first impressions, do they want to have a neon sign flashing from their nose saying, "There's something kind of strange about me. Just be warned."

Relationships with good, trustworthy human beings are hard to form. Do you want to scare them with your piercings? Or do you want to reassure them that you might be a good, reliable friend and lover?

Maybe it's just me. I am 66 years old as I am writing this, so maybe I am just out of date. But when I see a neatly dressed, clean, well-groomed man or woman, that's who I am likely to hire, to trust, to help out when he is in need.

Or when she is in need.

Again, you only get one chance to make a first impression. Yes, maybe in eighth grade it's cool to look weird, or maybe in eleventh grade. But when you are out in the work force, out where you have to get your back into your living, you might wish to look as normal as possible. The men and women who get hired, who get friends and lovers, generally— not always—get them based on first impressions. Nose piercings do not help.

Neither do long, scraggly beards or facial jewelry or anything that speaks of pain and disorganization. Generally speaking, and with some exceptions, when men and women are well-groomed, clean-shaven, have on clean and neat clothes, they look much more as if they could be counted on to get the job done—as worker, friend, or lover.

I am well aware of the temptation to use one's appearance to shock and attack those around us. I did it myself when I was a student. It didn't work well for me in what was then my career as a trial lawyer. It did, however, help me get noticed by the girls. But *getting girls* is only a small part of the life of even a semi-responsible adult. And in any event, I didn't have any piercings or tattoos or anything out of the ordinary in the way men looked in 1972. Even Nixon and Bob Haldeman had long sideburns.

By the way . . . as I think about this, I find myself thinking about the way human beings look in America, or at least in Southern California, generally in the present day.

They often look as if they have been through some kind of apocalypse. They look bedraggled and beaten. They look shaggy and confused and menacing. Many of the young people and their elders look as if they are purposely seeking to make themselves look ugly. The amazing part, to me, is that the most posh neighborhoods often have the most horrible-looking people. I wonder what happened. In Malibu in particular, some of the most well-to-do and successful people look the most, well, let's say, *primitive*.

But this isn't just Malibu or Southern California. All over the nation and the world, men and women look like slobs, except in small swaths of New York City, Washington, DC, and Boston. What happened? I guess it was the stress of the nuclear age or maybe of the sexual revolution.

To go back to Malibu, where I have a very modest home, I often see people in my nearby grocery store who I am sure are homeless. They look straggly and unkempt. They look lost and fearful and dangerous.

Routinely, after they go out the door of the grocery store, they get into Bentleys, Porsches, Mercedes, and Aston Martins. It isn't even unusual any longer.

What can this mean? When did people who can afford to look any way they want decide to look like homeless street people?

And what about people at the airport? I am sure that any reader under 50 cannot imagine it, but men and women used to dress up for travel. The men wore suits and ties. The women wore suits and stockings and high-heeled shoes. When did this change so that the people milling at the gates for LAX look like inmates of a particularly impoverished state's mental hospital?

Anyway, if you talk to women in confidence, as I do all day, they will tell you they like for men to be dressed neatly in a suit and tie. Men certainly like for women to look well dressed and well coiffed. Whoever told college girls to travel with dirty hair and in sweatshirts was not doing them a favor. What possible good can it do for a college girl to walk through an airport looking like a homeless person, inevitably clutching a pillow?

I can sum this up. Too often, men and women look scary and off-putting. They look as if they do not want to be hired, to be loved, or to be friends. They do not have to look like that. If they want to make a statement, let them write a manifesto. Or if they want to show they're rebels, let them rob a bank (just kidding about that one). But there is just no good reason to put on a fright face/hair/clothing outfit that can only succeed in lowering your income, status, or charm, and make you lonely. Don't do it. Look normal. Look middle class and boring and lovely, and do your rebelling while you're horizontal.

24

Save and Beware

As the day wore on at the set where we were shooting the commercial, I was in a tiny little snippet about a game of tennis. In the snippet, a fat, old, opinionated Ben Stein was getting tennis lessons from a properly dressed, fit-looking tennis pro. The actor playing the tennis pro did his work competently and then was *wrapped* as we say, and allowed to collect his belongings, sign his papers for his day's pay, and go home.

As he was packing up, one of the commercial's producers whispered to me that the actor was none other than BLANK, a truly giant singing star of my youth. This man was in a singing group that was enormous—wildly successful when I was in high school and for many years afterwards. Now, he's doing daywork as an actor in a commercial at a truly modest wage.

It reminded me of years ago when I was shopping for a Toyota at a car dealership in North Hollywood (not a posh neighborhood at all), and my salesman turned out to have been the lead backup singer and lead guitar for an immensely successful rock group of the 60s and 70s: Tommy James and the Shondells. Now, he was selling me a Celica Supra.

To be sure, there was nothing at all desperate about the former singing star on the set a few days ago. But people who could be at the country club do not usually do daywork on a commercial. It is totally honest work, and it's important work, as is selling cars. But it's not the kind of work that a man who earned and banked big checks and behaved sensibly around money usually does. (The recording star at the car dealership died while I was in negotiations with him over a second Toyota that I was only going to buy because I liked the man.)

I see this kind of story constantly in my little life. People who were once making the big dollar turned out to be hard up as they grew older. There were many of them in my extended family. Many of my friends have turned out to be such people. They are often fine people. They lived well, but did not save

137

or develop backup means of earning a living. I know their way of life well. I could easily see myself being one of them, I am sorry to say.

To spend money as fast and faster than you get it is a commonplace of life, especially for me.

To ride a big, juicy wave of money when you're young and expect that ride to continue all of your life is a commonplace of life.

To invest poorly and inadequately is also a commonplace of life.

To have your career turn out totally worse than you thought it would is a commonplace of life.

There is a big lesson here. Life is uncertain. That means that when the getting is good, it's time to save. Life is full of twists and turns that you least expect. That means that when you can, you should save.

Let me offer a couple of small examples from my own little life.

Long ago, when I was a speechwriter for Richard Nixon, I was only 28 years old. I thought I would set Washington, DC, on fire. At the urging of my then girlfriend, I bought a home in a nice neighborhood called Wesley Heights. By today's standards, my salary was tiny ($25,000) and the home was virtually free ($55,000). But it was a lot to me, and I was nervous about it. My girlfriend demanded that I buy the house though, and with every instinctual alarm bell ringing, I bought the house.

Within months, I had lost my job at the White House, just as Mr. Nixon did, and I was in a total panic about money. Luckily, I got through it alive, but I was really scared.

Much more recently, as my *acting* career was starting, I booked one job after another and seemed to be headed for permanent star status. I can vividly recall, as if it were yesterday, an article about me as a successful character actor in Hollywood. It came out in about 1992 or 1993. It said that if Hollywood wanted a teacher or a doctor or a judge or anyone boring, the go-to actor was Ben Stein. That article was in the *New York Times*.

After that article appeared, I did not get an acting job for years. Luckily, I had saved and did not go hungry.

The world is a roller coaster. You can keep from falling off, onto the rails, and getting your head cut off (as a high school classmate of mine, Eddie Rothbard, did at Glen Echo amusement park in the distant past) by having savings. This is as important as anything else in your life.

When the getting is good, you should save money. Don't fail to do this. The day will come when you'll need it.

And when you do save it, save it in a highly diversified form. Do not just think that because you have a home, you can consider that a piggy bank for the long-term future. Real estate can crash, as we have learned not once but many times. If you think you can always cash out, think again.

Stocks by themselves won't do it either. The most diversified portfolio can come to ruin—at least for a time.

You need cash and a home and stocks—maybe a little bit of a commodities fund in there, too. So, save and be diversified. Then you can do the little bits of acting with Ben Stein, and then go back to the country club and tell the story.

25

Play It Safe

THE NEXT ACT in the drama on that set of the commercial came when I picked up my trusty Verizon Voyager to call one of my very dearest friends. He sounded badly beaten down, out of breath, and weary. I asked him what the matter was. After a number of hesitating hems and haws, he told me he was in trouble with the law.

To make a cruelly long discussion short, he has been indicted on about a dozen felony counts of securities fraud. That is serious business.

Now my legal vineyard is securities law. I had the honor of studying it under Jan Deutsch at Yale Law School. I taught it for many years at Pepperdine Law School. But most of all, I wrote long, detailed articles about if for *Barron's* for a considerable period of years.

I hope to say I know securities law. Based on that knowledge, and the need for there to be some intent for a crime to have been committed, I do not for one instant believe my pal committed a single breach of criminal law. I am sure the prosecuting attorney means well and is a highly competent attorney. But I know the facts of the case a bit, and I simply do not see a real violation of law. I will spare you the details, but there just was no intent to defraud. I do not see that at all.

I do see careless conduct by a businessman who borrowed money and then got slammed by the recession and could not pay it back. I do see a dear friend who was trying his best to run his business, largely with borrowed money, as is commonplace with businesses, and got caught in a maelstrom of economic calamity. That was not his fault. The whole world got caught off guard by the credit crunch.

But my friend should nevertheless have been more careful. He should have set aside money not just for bad times, but for disastrously bad times. He behaved reasonably for the context of his young life, but not for the whole palette of dismal, dark colors one encounters in whirlwinds of the economy.

There is another lesson there: Do not just plan for bad. Plan for the very, very worst.

It can happen, and it will happen, unless it doesn't. Even then, you'll be happy you have the money in the bank.

Plus, you will not have to worry about getting those annoying communications from the Attorney General. Having enough money in bad times is one of the best things you can have.

26

Be Nice

THE FINAL LESSON of that day was an uplift. The persons who own the company for whom I did the commercial are super-loveable people. They are from the Rocky Mountains. They have no pretensions about them at all. They thought of a much-needed product. They did not just moon about trying to get it off the ground. They just took themselves to modest offices and went to work. Now they have a successful business. If our Internet commercial works well, maybe their business will be more successful, and maybe some kindly souls will come along and buy their business. Maybe they'll not sell and just keep expanding their business.

Now these guys are not Warren Buffett. They're not Henry Ford. They are smart guys who got off their butts and did something. They are entrepreneurs.

More than that, however, they are genuine geniuses of personality. They get along amazingly well with everyone whose path they cross—and everyone loves them. Everyone wants to be in business with them and to be their pal. (Well, not *everyone*, but many people.)

The *secret* to their success is that they play well with others—and they actually get things done.

Plus they have another *secret* to their success: They have a plan. They do not just go from day to day thinking about how to get through the day (although for some people, that works well, too). They had a plan with day-by-day steps to get from point A to point B and then to Point Success.

The upshot had been success.

Warren E. Buffett, my mentor and guide, has written that " . . . an idiot with a plan can beat a genius without a plan. . . . " These men and women were extremely smart people who also had a plan. That was a big part of their success.

To be sure, some plans make no sense and might as well be cheesecloth. But having a general idea of where you want to go, and how you want to get there, and what the intermediate steps are—and then taking those steps—these are a big part of the way to success.

Of course, to many people, just getting through the day without hurting themselves with drugs or alcohol or violence, or just getting through the day without *devastating blows of low self-esteem* as a long-ago friend said to me, is a great way to spend the day.

But for other more ambitious souls, a fine way to start the day is to realize where you are on your plan—for a new business, to win the woman of your dreams, to get into the college of your choice, to buy the home of your fantasies—check that against your plan, and try to move forward according to plan.

27

Thoughts on the Economic Morass and How to Get Out of It

Now, just to throw you a curveball, we are going to enter the world of policy for a few moments and talk about the state of the economy in America today.

We can start, as we should, with the obvious.

We have many economic problems in America today. We have an economy that is slowly recovering from a financial crisis. The crisis was man-made. It was not a tsunami following an earthquake as we witnessed in Japan in March of 2011. It was a man-made disaster caused by greedy and irresponsible behavior at big and small banks and incredibly incompetent behavior at the federal regulatory level.

For the bankers to have been as reckless and greedy as they were is almost impossible to believe. For them to have shoveled money into loans that had scant chance of being repaid, but which yielded immense short-term fees, was suicidal greed and shortsighted. For them to have sold baskets of these worthless—or nearly worthless—loans to unions; municipalities; foreign buyers; and above all, to the US taxpayer; was a fraud on a staggering scale. The truth that, as of this writing in the summer of 2011, not one man or woman has gone to prison for this malfeasance, is deeply disturbing.

Either the government is in the pocket of these questionable banks and individuals or it is too supine to energetically pursue the people responsible. In either case, the government is not functioning well.

It gets worse, because for the powers that be in the federal government to have been as incompetent as they were about not rescuing Lehman Brothers—an immense bank with large, vulnerable *long* positions in mortgage-backed securities . . . when it was about to fail—that was mind-boggling.

Lesson one, for any financial regulator, is that you simply do not allow a major bank to fail in a financial crisis. This has been obvious since 1931, when the federal government let a large private bank, The Bank of The United States, fail. It was that failure, more than any other single event, which precipitated the Great Depression. Responsible governments simply do not allow big banks to fail in times of financial peril. To allow such a failure sends panic through the entire economy. That is precisely what happened with Lehman. We don't know why, exactly, the government allowed it to happen. Seemingly, a mixture of personality problems on the part of the Chairman of the Board of Governors of the Federal Reserve System, Dr. Ben Bernanke, and the then Secretary of the Treasury, Henry Paulson, was involved. But for whatever reason, we had that inexcusably foolish move by the government, and we got a financial panic.

Luckily we are now recovering, in some areas more quickly than others. It has been a bloody time. The financial meltdown cost investors and savers trillions. The bailouts and assorted stimulus packages cost more than a trillion dollars. The debt that has been run up in an effort to stanch the bleeding in the economy threatens to overwhelm the entire financial system of this country. It is not at all clear that there is any long-term way to avoid default on the debt of the United States of America either directly (very unlikely) or indirectly through inflating away the debt. That is, the government would create so much inflation that the size of the debt, in current dollars, would fall to a manageable level compared with tax revenues. This would be a mammoth cheat on the American saver, investor, and retiree, but it could well happen.

Your humble servant hopes that by the time you read this, we will at last be in a full recovery, even in housing—the hardest-hit area. As I am writing this, employment is picking up slowly, and there are a few feeble hints of light in the housing darkness.

But again, we do seem to have the makings of a recovery. The takeaway here is that there are a lot of imperfect people operating in the world of money, and that we had better have our own stash—and we had better keep a close eye on it.

We have learned we cannot trust the men with the silk hats, and we cannot trust the propellorheads, and we cannot trust the bureaucrats. We have to be able to trust ourselves and one or two close personal financial advisors, and that's enough. We will get into choosing a financial advisor soon.

"God bless the child that's got his own," goes the spiritual, and we had better work hard to be that child.

28

Progress, Not Perfection

OF COURSE, WE have foreign relations problems and problems with Islamic terrorists, too. Just as I am writing this, the US Navy SEALs killed Osama bin Laden, which is cause for rejoicing. But there are plenty of others like him out there, just as evil and sick. This is going to be a problem for a very long time.

And we have the continuing, unending problem of racism. This is possibly just a basic part of human nature, but in any event, it's getting a great deal better. I will get to that in more detail later, but suffice it to say for right now that America is an incomparably kinder, gentler nation as far as racism goes than it was 50 years ago.

Fifty years ago, lynchings were not terribly unusual in the Deep South. Eighty years ago, they were not unusual in the Midwest. Now they almost never happen. The idea that man will be wary of other men because of their race or skin color may be around for a while, but we are blessed that the blemish of racism is not making people kill each other on the basis of race now in this country.

That is a true miracle of change in this America. Paid for with blood. Paid for with civil rights workers' blood, with Medgar Evers's blood, with Dr. Martin Luther King, Jr.'s blood, but now we have a nation where legalized racism no longer exists, and the law offers no sanction for racial violence.

So that problem will be around in some people's hearts for awhile, but as a national problem of a legal structure empowering the feelings of racism, it is vanishing.

What would Ben do about that? He would be, and is, on his knees endlessly thanking God that racism is a far smaller problem than it used to be.

A great many of our problems are getting better, and racism—a vicious curse on mankind—is one of them.

29

Education—To Read or Not to Read

BUT THERE ARE some problems that are not getting better. One of the main problems that seems to me to lurk as a national—and individual—problem with no bottom is education.

We have gone from being one of the best-educated nations in the world to being a basket case of education in a very short time.

The statistics are dreadful.

Our students routinely come in last, or close to last, on worldwide tests in math and science taken in developed nations. Our students' ability to know even the most basic facts of history is pitifully limited.

A recent study by the ACT said that only one-fourth of high school seniors would be capable of doing C-level work in college. Frankly, C-level work in college today is not impressive. A very recent study, as I am writing this in the spring of 2011, has said that a large number of college sophomores know less about history and literature than they did when they were high school seniors.

To this must—sadly—be added my own anecdotal experience as a teacher and observer.

I meet not just some, but many young people who simply do not know the basics of history. They don't know when the Civil War was. They don't know when the Declaration of Independence was. They have no idea of what The Bill of Rights is or what its purpose was and is. They don't know what *Brown v. Board of Education* was. They don't know what the struggle for civil rights for African Americans and for women was about or how costly it was.

They don't know who we fought against in World War II. They don't know who our allies were in World War II. They don't know where on the map France and Britain are.

They know far too little.

Knowledge is vital. It is vital to keep a free people free. As Jefferson said, "Whoever expects a people to remain free in a state of ignorance expects what never was and never will be."

Speaking of which, just a few days ago, I showed a woman friend a photo of Jefferson Davis and asked her who he was. The woman is a PhD in divinity from a major university.

"Well," she said, "I cheated. I can see under your hand that it's Thomas Jefferson."

"No, it's not," I told her. "It's Jefferson Davis."

"Who the heck is he?" she asked.

"He was the president of the Confederacy," I said. "The southern states that seceded in the Civil War."

"In what way did they succeed?" she asked brightly.

"I didn't they say *succeeded*," I said. "They seceded. They left the Union. And they tried to form a country, and their president was Jefferson Davis."

"So, then who was Thomas Jefferson?" she asked. And she has a PhD.

I would not be deeply worried if the issue were names and dates, although they are important, too. The more frightening problem is that young and old Americans do not know what sets this nation apart.

They do not know that we are the first nation to be founded on the principle of government by consent of the governed. They do not know how rare genuine, individual freedom is in the world even today. They have no idea of how much blood has been shed to keep America free. And, what is even worse, they don't seem to care. They seem to believe that freedom and the protection of law is their birthright and will always be theirs for the taking.

This is a catastrophe in the works. It is indispensable to Americans to know how blessed and fortunate we are to be America and to live in the state of freedom under law in which we find ourselves.

If we do not understand how crucial freedom is to us, if we do not understand the horror that is life in despotism, we can lose our freedom and go the way of despotism. If we do not understand how much blood and pain and death have been expended to keep us free, we will never be willing to sacrifice again to keep ourselves free.

This whole country is like the story of the rich heir who was born on third base and thought he had hit a triple. We did not, do not, deserve our happy fate—and we won't keep it for long—unless and until we understand how precious it is and how costly it is to preserve it.

Knowledge has immense economic value as well.

The nation with the most capital will, other things being equal, be the richest nation. Capital can be land or resources or ports. And these are valuable resources indeed as capital. Just look at the stunning wealth of the oil exporters and you get an idea of how big a part resources play in the wealth of nations.

But the author of the definitive book on economics, the most important book on human organization ever written, Adam Smith, who wrote *The Wealth of Nations*, had a bigger and better idea about where the true wealth of nations comes from.

Adam Smith said that the real, lasting wealth of nations comes from the industriousness, energy, imagination, and education of its people. In Adam Smith's mind, education was at the very pinnacle of these assets.

Without education, no nation could be a wealthy nation—at least not for long.

This was his theory, and it made a lot of sense.

There is a study to the same effect with a bit more precision. Roughly 50 years ago, one of the great geniuses of economics, Edward Denison, wrote a pioneering study to attempt to quantify this issue of the economic value of education. He wrote a book called *The Sources of Economic Growth*. I know that book and knew it at birth, because in a youthful summer job, I worked in an office and proofread the galleys of that book.

Not at all surprisingly, Ed Denison found that education was an immense factor in any nation's economic growth.

That factor propelled the United States into the stratosphere of prosperity in the twentieth century, especially after 1945. We reached new highs, year after year, in educational attainment.

We became the scientific and technological leader of the world by an immense amount and on that, built phenomenal wealth.

There was a direct link between our national prosperity and our national education, and that link worked to raise our national standard of living to a level that would have been unimaginable even in the 1920s.

Then something happened. The trends in educational achievement stalled, and then went slowly, and then went rapidly into reverse. As we all know—and as I just wrote—scores on achievement tests fell. Employers had difficulty, and still have difficulty, finding qualified hires in the technical and mathematical fields. Little by little, the balance of educational power began to tilt toward the Far East. The educational machine in this country sputtered and sputters still, while Asia races forward.

Now it is a total myth that all of those people in Asia are all born great at math and physics and are born knowing electrical engineering. They have their share of problem students and problem workers, too. India, which graduates hundreds of thousands of engineers each year, has difficulty finding enough of them who can do serious work to fill its outsourcing centers for US clients.

But that's their problem.

Our problem is that we as a nation are not turning out well-educated young people the way we used to and the way we need to.

We do not exactly know why.

Part of the problem may be that many school systems abandoned memorization and serious study in favor of a curriculum that supposedly makes students " . . . feel good about themselves . . . " until they have to find a job.

Part of the problem may be that we have so many students for whom English is not their native language and not the language that is spoken in the home. It is hard to learn in a foreign language. Just for me, I doubt I could do it at all.

Another huge part of the problem is that we have in the school system far too many students whose home life is not ideal. They have single parents or no parents at all. Their neighborhoods are dangerous. There are gangs and drugs at their schools. The children in a distressed urban neighborhood come to school each day with a load of problems on their backs that would be unimaginable to a child with two well-to-do parents and a warm, nurturing home environment.

A child who must contend with drug dealers nearby and the sound of gunfire will have an entirely different burden than a boy or girl from Scarsdale or Beverly Hills.

Plus there is the problem of teachers. Teaching is no longer a plum job for many Americans. It is no longer where the best and brightest routinely want to be, although to be sure, many of the very smartest still do want to teach. But too many teachers are just bored bureaucrats. They teach because they have job security (or did until recently) and great health and pension benefits (or did until recently). Too many of them lack the zeal necessary to be great pedants.

There are obviously many other causes that we have not figured out yet. Possibly the popular culture belittles education and offers up contempt for those who study and learn well. Possibly the spectacular pay and perks of sports stars and entertainers dazzles young people out of serious, sustained effort to work at normal jobs.

Or, possibly, we just got too fat and pimpled and lazy. "I need a job and I'll work for it," got replaced by, "Take your job and shove it." So did education. A healthy and sane respect for learning got replaced by, "We don't need no education. We don't need no thought control . . . hey, teachers, leave them kids alone."

So, what do we do?

One approach that might have merit is the attempt to automate and at the same time customize learning through online teaching.

Today, for many young people, the Internet IS their family. They can relate better to the computer screen than they can to real, live teachers or to their *friends*, if they have any friends, or to their families. To today's child, the Internet is the route to the place they want to be.

What if we could take the Internet and put the very best teachers we have on it, and diffuse their knowledge throughout the nation and the world? What if we could take truly great teachers, with great curricula, and make their knowledge and wisdom available to every child who wanted to learn?

That is what you can do online.

Parents are often absent or too concerned with their own problems to remind students of their work and their duties to read material and do their papers.

What if the Internet teacher/parent/friend could remind the student to do his or her work? And keep reminding him or her until it got done?

It is happening right now.

What if the Internet could monitor a student's term paper as he was writing it, and correct it, and make suggestions for improvement?

It is happening right now.

What if every lesson, in every subject, could be accompanied by graphics and illustrations of previously unthinkable appeal and richness?

It is happening right now and will happen more in the future.

The software for this kind of miraculous change in education is getting smarter and smarter every day. It is becoming literally self-aware. Programmers can tell it—just in general terms—what to do, and the software will improve itself.

Now this is just at the beginning.

The addition of the power of the Internet to the power of the soul of a great teacher is leading us to a sum which just might stop the agonizing slide of much of this country into ignorance.

Obviously, this approach will not work for everyone. And some will rightly say that to make homework like watching an interactive video game is simply making it too easy and taking away the discipline that is itself a big part of the educational process.

There will be children whose burdens of alienation are so weighty that even the most appealing of online experiences will not lure them in.

But the challenge we face educationally is overwhelming. We should be using every single possible tool in the workshop to improve things. If online learning is one of those tools, and if the software and hardware are already here—why not go for it?

Then there is another plus: Much of the online learning that goes on in this country now is at for-profit schools. Some educators look down upon these schools, and there have certainly been abuses in the field—especially where federal dollars have been in play. Too often some of these schools have been funnels for taking money from taxpayers and giving it to proprietors, with the students coming in second or third.

But there are also top-notch for-profit schools that turn out grads who get what they want: training to do a specific job and to move from manual labor or unemployment to middle class status. These schools may not turn out philosophers or film critics. But they do generate tens of thousands of graduates who get jobs as nurses, hospital administrators, engineers, accountants, and other useful and necessary occupations.

These schools, again, are for-profit. That means they have an immense incentive to make education actually work for the graduates. Otherwise, the word gets around for students to avoid that school. They also have a motive to be more efficient. They are not guaranteed existence into perpetuity like public schools or well-endowed private universities. They exist and thrive if they get people educated and if they can do it at a price.

But this happens to be exactly what society in general wants: graduates who can do their jobs and who get educated at a price the society can afford.

One source of this happy product will be online learning. Your humble servant, *moi*, has seen this process at work—and it works. It may only be one answer, but it is an answer. And we are in such a state that we need every answer we can find.

30

The Good Side of Drugs

Now let's stay in this public policy world for a moment and talk about drugs and health care.

As I am writing this, the nation is still in the throes of a vast debate about health care. Obamacare has passed and been signed. It has not been implemented yet, except at a superficial level, but there are many efforts afoot to repeal it.

Frankly, I don't see how those efforts can possibly succeed with a Democratic President and a Democratic Senate, but maybe something will happen that I don't yet foresee.

We do know for sure that we have a health care crisis. Just to start with extremely basic points, we have too many Americans lacking health insurance and unable to get decent care except in haphazard ways.

At the same time, we have too little money available to the government of this country to pay for a vast expansion of health care coverage without gravely endangering our already dicey budgetary and national debt problems.

Plus we have the problem that there is a shortage of qualified doctors and that much of their time is now taken up with the minutiae of filling out forms rather than actually caring for the health of their patients.

We also have a stunning quantum of unqualified doctors passing out health care that harms far more than it helps. (I often think of the old saw: "What do you call the lowest-ranking graduate of the worst medical school in the world?" Answer: "Doctor.")

How will we solve this problem? One way is a one-syllable word: drugs.

Now let's back up for a moment and get to some basics.

The absolutely least expensive way to deal with the problems of medical costs is prevention.

If every American would eat a bit less sugar, meat, saturated fats, and salt, we would have a considerably lessened national health care problem. Most of my diet consists of exactly these foods, and they have made me fat, so I can testify to their negative effects.

If each American would take some daily exercise and move his or her body vigorously for some good part of the day, we would have a far smaller health problem and far smaller expenses on medical care. I can also say I exercise a lot each day in my swimming pool, and it invariably makes me feel better. So there is some anecdotal evidence in addition to the vast libraries of more scientific data on the subject.

Seriously, exercise of even a modest amount is a fantastic godsend to the human body, even fat, old bodies like mine.

If each American were to get a flu shot every year, we would have a far healthier America. Ditto with pneumonia shots and colonoscopies.

If everyone drove the speed limit and wore seat belts, we would have a far healthier America. If no one drank to excess or used illegal narcotics, we would have a much reduced burden on our health care system. If every American got enough sleep, that small step by itself would make a difference. We humans are far more susceptible to disease when fatigued. We are far more likely to have auto accidents and other accidents when exhausted. And we are incomparably more likely to have mental health problems when excessively tired.

If no one skateboarded, that would also be a big health plus.

Prevention is extremely inexpensive and would save truly staggering sums. That should be our number one priority for efficient savings in health care.

The most expensive way to deal with the health issue is to have every patient who is ill or injured go to a hospital emergency room and demand care no matter whether he or she has health insurance. Hospital emergency room care is extremely costly and getting more so.

The second most expensive way to deal with health costs is to have everyone who is ill go to the doctor and have every kind of test and every kind of procedure that anyone in the doctor's family who needs a mink coat can think of.

Unfortunately, that is the system we have now. Once a patient gets into the clutches of a doctor or hospital, a D-Day armada of tests comes bearing down upon him or her.

Why not? The doctor gets paid for them. The hospital gets paid for them. They help ward off lawsuits. All costs are shuffled off onto insurers, insured patients, and the US taxpayer. So, why not have the tests? There is every incentive to have them ordered up by the score, and none for foregoing them and taking a more cautious approach.

Is there any way out?

Maybe. The most cost-effective way to deal with the nation's health care problems once an ailment has already begun is to have the patient use medicines, and use them first and fast instead of endless consumption of hospital, laboratory, and physician time. It just might work.

The mind of man has invented medicines that prevent disease, that treat disease, and that cure disease.

These are sometimes expensive compared with water from the tap. But compared with surgery or a continuing hospital stay, they are extremely cost effective.

The idea that medicines, and the pharmaceutical companies, and the companies that dispense medicines are the problem is just plain not true. They are the solution, not the problem.

Intelligently created, compassionately prescribed, carefully monitored with the help of the Internet, medicines are probably our very best bet after prevention in maintaining health care in a way we can afford as people and as a nation.

There has been one immensely useful solution to the basic human problem of *shortage* that has plagued mankind since the beginning of existence. That solution has been mass production.

Until mass production of food was made possible by scientific farming methods and mass production of quality farm implements and farm chemicals, mankind was in a chronic state of famine over much of the globe. After that, the problem changed so much that in much of the world, especially the Western world, the human nutrition problem is overeating and overfeeding.

Until the English and French commenced mass production of textiles in the eighteenth century and nineteenth century, mankind was chronically ill-clothed. Until mankind acquired the means of mass producing cotton and wool, and then synthetics, it was rare for a man to own more than one shirt. Now the homes of mankind in much of the world are stuffed with clothing that men and women buy, forget about, and hardly ever wear after the first use.

The same is true of housing. For most of man's time on this earth, each home or hut he and his family lived in had to be individually and painstaking assembled with each part handmade. This made living space extremely expensive for the ordinary citizen. It meant that families lived in extremely modest quarters, unless they were rich or at least well-to-do.

But when lumber and bricks began to be mass produced, when whole neighborhoods were assembled at once with the techniques of mass production, the relative cost of living space declined dramatically. The amount of square feet available to the ordinary American family is now phenomenally larger than it was even as recently as 1945—by some measurements, about three times as many square feet per family member larger.

Obviously, the same is true of automobiles and trucks.

In health care, there is only one area in which mass production can be applied to saving life and health: drugs (or medicines).

Once a medicine has been perfected, it can be manufactured in ever greater quantities with the same level of quality as in smaller quantities. Its production can be scaled up, as the modern expression goes, and costs can come down.

This is the only area of health care where modern techniques of mass production can work.

Obviously, patients cannot be wheeled around hospitals like cars on an assembly line. Patients are people with highly individual maladies and sensibilities. They have to be handled as handcrafted entities. But once their disease has been diagnosed, the treatment for that disease can be dispensed, with the savings that mass production of the drug allows.

This is—again—the only area where I can see techniques of mass production available to be used. It is important that we respect it and not hamstring it with excessive regulation or taxation.

Dispensing the medications in a sensible, intelligent way is also the key. The nation's pharmacies can work to buy sensibly, to dispense with thoughtfulness and care, in order to ensure that the patient/customer gets no more than he or she needs, at a price he or she can afford to pay. This, also, is a facet of mass production.

We don't need to engage in a war among drugmakers, the government, pharmacies, and patients. There is plenty of work for all of us to do, and plenty of money to be made in a legitimate and caring way. Using modern techniques of high quality, low price production is the key.

31

To the Tables Down at Mory's

However, there is a big, big exception about the incredible value of drugs, which I am about to get to. It has to do with the misprescribing of meds. Let's use me as an example:

It is morning here where I am writing this in Rancho Mirage, California. The sky is clear, and there is a slight breeze wafting through the palm trees. But for some unknown reason, I am thinking about grey New England mornings long ago when I was a law student at Yale Law School, from 1966 to 1970. Those were the days, my friend.

Those among my readers who are lawyers may now be thinking, "Hey, wait a minute. What's he talking about? Law school is three years, not four years. What's this nonsense? And anyway, what the heck does it have to do with medicines?"

Yes, law school is generally three years, but it took me four years, and thereby hangs a tale which may be of interest in several ways, and may offer some lessons, including about the misdiagnosis of patients and the mis-prescription of drugs.

As a senior in college, at Columbia, I was fortunate enough to get into all of the well-known law schools—Harvard, Yale, Columbia, University of Chicago, and Stanford.

I never seriously planned to go to Harvard, because I had heard it was rigorous and difficult. Besides, I find Cambridge, Massachusetts, a bit depressing in terms of climate and architecture. My plan was to go to Stanford, in beautiful Palo Alto, California.

I had visited Stanford that winter and loved the climate and the open, pleasant spaces. It looked good to me. Besides, my parents' dear friend, Milton Friedman, the greatest thinker I have ever met besides my father, had endorsed Stanford in a roundabout way. When I was thinking of going to business school, he had said to me, "You might as well go to Stanford.

You don't learn anything at any of them, and Stanford has the best climate."

I am sure he was mistaken about whether you learn anything in business schools, but Stanford surely has a fine climate.

That was enough for me. Or it would have been. . . .

But then my brother-in-law, Melvin Epstein, a successful Wall Street lawyer who had gone to Harvard and Harvard Law, had worked incredibly hard there, then incredibly hard at his major Wall Street firm, told me some choice words about Yale.

"It's a country club," he said. "You just loll around and at the end of three years, you get a diploma and because of the name *Yale*, you get a good job."

(This might have been a play on John F. Kennedy's famous words when he got an honorary degree at Yale in 1962. "Now," said JFK, "I have the best of both worlds: a Harvard education and a Yale degree.")

That sounded magically wonderful to me. I didn't want to do any more work than I absolutely had to. So off I went to Yale in September of 1966.

It was a disaster . . . an absolute nightmare.

After four years of being master of my classes at Columbia, with nary a difficult moment in learning any subject except physics (cruelly mis-titled *Physics for Poets* when it should have been called *torture*), I found law school totally mystifying. My very first class was in a subject called Federal Civil Procedure, taught by a great expert in that field: a little sadist named J. William Moore.

The very first case we read was a dense legal opinion about the difference between *collateral estoppel* and *res judicata*, two concepts that made no sense to me at all. The legal opinion was incomprehensible. Professor Moore's method of *explaining* it to us was to pick on one of the three of four women students in the class and tease and badger her until she cried and ran from the room. Then he did the same with the male students.

Our contracts teacher, a swaggering German named Kessler, was exactly the same, except with a thick German accent. When a poor, hapless student essayed an answer that the professor found incorrect, "Fritz" Kessler would say, with contempt so radioactive it could have fried Nagasaki, "You couldn't be wronger."

Constitutional law was taught by a chain-smoking nervous man named Charles Reich. He was a gentleman. He did not bully anyone, but neither did he explain one damned thing. At the time, he had become a celebrity by writing a hippie book about new consciousness called *The Greening of America*. He might as well have been speaking Chinese as talking about law in English.

The students at Yale were (I am sure) fine people, but they were not my cup of tea. They were as serious as a heart attack, totally driven and ambitious, and up for nothing but studying. I am sure they were, in their hearts, laughing, happy men and women. But their surface was intense and mirthless.

My roommate was a Midwesterner who never came out of his room after class, even for dinner, so as to make more time for study. I do not recall him ever exchanging a word with me.

I was a party animal. This law school was 10,000 times too serious for me. It was not even remotely the *country club* my brother had been talking about. It was much more like a ministry in *Nineteen Eighty-Four*.

I hated the classes, hated the homework, found no social life at all congenial to me, and detested the weather. I found myself overwhelmed with confusion and dismay. Plus I had two pretty girlfriends to squire around, and that took a lot of my time. I might as well have been Jerry Rubin in a physics class at M.I.T.

Soon I was seriously behind in my reading. That made me anxious. Plus, as noted, I didn't feel as if I fit in there. I went to the student medical clinic to talk to a psychiatrist about my anxiety about my studies. This cretin told me I would be fine and could do my work and catch up if I just took two little medicines: Trilafon and Mellaril. They would change my mood and make me a happy, productive scholar of the law.

I didn't know any better, so I took them. Little did I know that they were ultra-potent antipsychotics. Their recommended use was not for anxiety about studies, but for seriously psychotic patients in mental hospitals. Their list of cautions and side effects goes on for dozens of paragraphs. Some of the side effects, as I was to learn, were severe.

Soon I had devastating ailments, including dizziness, extreme fatigue, headaches, and a temporary paralysis of my back muscles so I could not walk and had to be taken to the Yale clinic by ambulance and given muscle relaxers.

A Better Day

Soon I was a hopeless, chain-smoking basket case. The meds had made me incomparably worse than I had been. I simply could not bear up any longer.

I arranged with an extremely kind associate dean by the name of Henry Varnum Poor, one of the noblest educators I have ever met, to take an indefinite leave of absence. He told me I could come back at any time.

I had only one friend in my class: a beautiful woman named Renee Poussaint. Only she showed any regret at my predicament, and only she seemed sad to see me go. I don't think my roommate, now a federal district court judge, even left his room to say good-bye as I drove off.

Soon I was back at home with my parents in Maryland, trying to figure out what to do with my pitiful life. My mother was furiously angry at me. My father was sympathetic.

Now I told you earlier what a lifesaving gift it was when my father urged me to go to work at a job, and thereby saved my sanity. The self-esteem of work will do that.

But leaving Yale Law when I did turned out to be one of the greatest blessings of a fantastically blessed life, and one that tells us humans something about our little lives.

Yes, those doctors were fools and knaves for giving me those drugs. Yes, my roommate was not much of a friend to me. Yes, I did not belong at Yale Law '69. Yes, again, while I am a wholehearted believer in medicines, the misuse of psychoactive medicines—and any other kind of medicines— can be deadly. But fate had a plan for me. While I was out of Yale, I worked first for a newsletter publisher, BNA, as described. Then I worked for the United States Department of Commerce as an economist. At that job, I worked in an anonymous, featureless office along an almost surreally long corridor. My job was to assemble a list of suggestions for those wishing to export to Canada. It was not bad work but hardly challenging. The worst part was that at the end of my corridor was a huge men's room. Whenever I visited it, it was filled with poor, frustrated, tormented bureaucrats suffering from loud and terrifying bouts of constipation and diarrhea.

The sounds and smells of the place somehow epitomized the essential futility and self-loathing of the bureaucratic life, as if the very bowels of these poor devils were in rebellion against their *lives*.

But outside of the toilet stalls, the people at Commerce were kind to me. Their insurance paid for my visits to a famous shrink named Robert N. Butler, MD, who recently died. They lavished praise on me. They told me I could be there forever. They paid me a whopping $125 a week.

But it was that Dante's *Inferno* men's room that told me I must get out of there. And it also told me that if I just never took those horrible meds or anything like them again, if I just found a roommate with one morsel of humanity, if I did not live on campus but off the Sterling Law Buildings pressure cooker grid, I could make a go of it at Yale Law School and have a shot at a better life. Certainly, ex-the drugs, ex-the roommate, and ex-the pressure cooker atmosphere in law school itself, there was hope.

Friends Indeed

And hope there turned out to be, indeed. The class of '70 was a totally different animal from the class of '69. The class of '69 was the last class from the *Silent Generation of the 1950s*. They wanted to be good boys and girls, to stay out of trouble, to keep quiet (silent), and to get decent jobs.

The class of '70 was rebels and hell-raisers—at least some of them. Enough of them were hippies and wise guys and men and women who did not take civil procedure seriously to make for a copious supply of friends.

From the first day of school, when I had lunch with a man who is still a friend, Bob Spearman, a high judge in North Carolina, I was blessed with pals. There was Duncan Kennedy, with his brilliant legal mind, and his hilarious wife, Mopsy. Duncan became a famed radical law professor at Harvard, always his life goal. There was Richard Balzer, radical and wit, and John W. Keker, Vietnam War Marine and hero, and now one of the great trial lawyers on this nation. There was Bob Calhoun, fresh from the Peace Corps in Turkey. Along with his wife, Susan, my wife and I played bridge with the Calhouns night after night, high as kites, laughing and a-singing until the early hours of the morn. I believe that even now, those nights at bridge with the Calhouns were the happiest social nights of my life.

There was Peter Broderick, film aficionado, with whom I worked on The Yale Law School Film Society, selecting movies to show, and bringing famous directors like Godard and Fritz Lang and Russ Meyer to Yale. Many an afternoon Peter and I wandered around the campus putting up posters for our movies and talking about film. Taking tickets at the film showings—admission was either 25 or 50 cents depending on one's age—was the best job I ever had. The meetings of the Film Society were as interesting and lively discussions as I have ever been privileged to attend.

There were my neighbors in New Haven: Chris Wilson and his fabulously beautiful and entertaining wife, Ruth. I have never laughed so hard in my life as I did at Chris's imitations of Hollywood stars. (His father was a successful screenwriter.)

Even the teachers seemed better the second time around. I was blessed to have a great Evidence teacher, Larry Simon, a super Labor Law teacher, Harry Wellington, and probably the best Constitutional Law teacher there was on the planet, Bob Bork, later cruelly denied his rightful place on the Supreme Court by a vengeful and unwell Ted Kennedy.

Most wonderful of all, by a pure gift from God, the faculty of the law school allowed us to take classes in other parts of the graduate schools at Yale and receive law school credit.

This allowed me to take two fine film courses from Stanley Kauffman, former film critic of the *New York Times,* and a genuinely great mind. I was also able to take several courses in the graduate school of economics from the immortal Henry Wallich, a truly important thinker in fiscal and monetary policy, and James Tobin, one of the geniuses of finance.

The life I had at Yale Law School was simply better than even my life at Columbia, which itself had been a mind-bogglingly great life of parties and dancing and drinking and night clubs and classes from C. Lowell Harriss, the single best teacher of economics or anything else I have ever had.

It was fantastically great . . . the stuff of dreams.

Now, before I go further with this story, please allow me to draw two immediate conclusions.

Psychiatrists who prescribe drugs are extremely dangerous instrumentalities. Not always. Psychoactive drugs are often helpful but often dangerous. The shrinks and other physicians who toss them around casually are irresponsible at best. Before you take them, hesitate a really long time, and desperately try to think of an alternative. The human brain is a delicate organ. When you seek to boss it around with medicines, you can get disastrous results.

Think of all the TV ads you have seen for antidepressants, tranquilizers, and sleep medications. Think of all the warnings they give: can cause suicide, can cause panic, can cause wild mood swings. Those warnings are there for a reason. Pay attention, and stay away if you can.

I have seen suicide attempts and one suicide from improper psychoactive medication. Approach this whole subject with utmost care.

Second, when you are with a group of people who are totally uncongenial, as I was when I first entered Yale Law School, it may not be you who is crazy. It might be that they are just so different from you that it makes no sense to try to fit in.

You are who you are. You should not have to put yourself into a contortion to be someone you are not. You just might not be meant to be there. Not everyone is meant to be in law school. Not everyone is meant to be anywhere. And just because someone tells you a place is a country club, that does not make it a country club.

The Gates of Eden

But there is a third lesson. Sometimes God, or fate, or whatever, picks you up and places you exactly where you are supposed to be.

My brother-in-law was right about Yale Law School. It was beyond a country club. It was a huge, nonstop party—and I learned a lot about how law works and how films work and how the economy works. It was pure pleasure and as it recedes ever farther into the past, it seems better and better.

Great things can happen, and life can be bliss. But when it isn't, you are in the wrong place at the wrong time. Get moving.

32

Tax Policy

HA! TALK ABOUT strange sex habits!

For most of America's life as a nation, we observed a sensible policy of spending and taxation. The underlying notion was that the government would not spend more than it took in from taxation.

This was an incredibly basic idea that made a lot of sense. Of course, there were times (such as during wars) when government had to spend more than it took in from taxation, but those instances were rare. The generally agreed-upon notion was that over any meaningful period of time, the federal budget had to be balanced. Taxes and spending had to be about the same. That was true under both parties and in every kind of situation except wars—and even then, the budget had to be balanced after the wars were over.

Then along came what was probably the worst idea in the history of free nations: supply side economics.

This idea, proposed by a genial, likeable fellow named Arthur Laffer, stated that if the federal government drastically lowered tax rates, this would stimulate the economy so much that it would boom—and that even with the lower rates, the government would collect more revenue than it did when tax rates were higher.

Now here comes the interesting part. There was *never any evidence at all* that this was true.

Let's be fair. The ultimate book of economics—*The Wealth of Nations*—had no collected data of any serious magnitude that would have gotten Adam Smith a degree in econometrics. It was based on incredibly acute observation of a small number of what we today call *data points*. But it was so sharply observed—and so consistent with what has turned out to be reality—that it has been considered the Bible of economics since 1776. (By the way, the three greatest works of writing ever struck off by the human mind—the Declaration of Independence, *The Wealth of Nations*, and *The Decline and Fall of the Roman Empire*—were all written and published within months of each other, without the Internet, without Google, and without electricity. To my mind, there is just no question that human beings were smarter at that time. I do not know why. By the way, that is within a few decades of when the other greatest works of man—the Constitution, as well as the music of Mozart and Beethoven—were written and published. As I said, people were smarter then.)

But back to supply side.

There never was any data showing that tax cuts would stimulate the economy enough to offset revenue losses to the federal government. It was just a pipe dream.

It was possible that the tax cuts *could* stimulate economic activity. But to fuel such growth to the point that it generated more revenue than it lost would have been virtually impossible.

The economy can grow in two ways: either by adding more man-hours to the labor supply, which raises total output but tends to lower output per worker—as the new hires tend to be less productive due to lack of experience. Or, the growth would come from greater worker productivity, which would happen if there were some important technological breakthrough like the steam engine or the railroad.

But the data is clear that productivity per worker hour has hardly grown at all in the past several decades, despite astonishing improvements in technology and those immense tax cuts. And, "hours worked" has barely budged.

Some say that supply side works by increasing the supply of capital. Thus there is more capital to work with, and worker productivity should therefore rise.

But the data is clear that—once again—worker productivity has not risen at an accelerated rate since the era of supply side began, in the 1980s.

More important—capital is a worldwide commodity that is available to rent from any quarter of the globe. China is amassing capital at a phenomenal rate, which it will lend to the United States or to anywhere else in the developed world for an extremely modest rate. The oil-producing states have massive amounts of capital they will lend out. There is no shortage of capital—so the aspect of supply side that states that there is has turned out to be utterly irrelevant. Lowering taxes does not add to capital or to productivity at any measurably meaningful rate.

And in fact, by generating such immense deficits as it has, supply side has actually sucked capital *out* of more productive uses and into buying government debt (although a large part of federal government debt is just financed with the printing press through Federal Reserve purchases . . . and again, capital is endlessly recirculated, so that if it does go into buying government debt, it can come out later as a factory). Still, capital is only meaningful as it adds to productivity, and that meaningful addition has not yet happened—alas.

Now some will say that the efficacy of supply side is shown by the fact that federal revenues were higher at the end of the Reagan years than before he cut taxes. That would be a good argument—except that in fact, Ronald Reagan raised taxes for six of his eight years in office—sometimes quite substantially. If we wanted to emulate Mr. Reagan, at this point we would raise taxes, just as he had the guts to do.

The *cut-taxes* crowd and the *deficits don't matter* crew are seeing the results of their well-meaning but deeply mistaken handiwork.

Mr. George W. Bush, a wonderful, kindly, good-natured and intelligent man—a true prince of a gentleman—inherited a sound budget and tax policy from his predecessor, Bill Clinton. He had a recession and a stock market crash to deal with. He had a defense challenge, or at least he thought he did.

Next thing we knew, he was cutting taxes like wildfire and raising government spending, especially on defense, like another wildfire.

The results were predictable. We got much higher deficits and a federal debt that was stupendously larger than had been anticipated when those tax cuts went into effect.

Then we got the financial panic of 2008–2009, a direct result of human incompetence at the Treasury and the Federal Reserve. This led to a severe recession. These slow-downs always cut into individual and corporate tax revenue, and so they did this time as well.

Soon we had a deficit under Mr. Barack Obama that made the Bush era deficits look modest.

Now it's the summer of 2011. As your humble servant writes this, we were in serious danger of spending so much and taking in so little that we would just blow right past the federal debt limit. In that case, we risked a default on interest payments on federal debt. On the one hand, we had a last minute deal that avoided default on our federal debt. On the other hand, we had a major ratings firm downgrade our sovereign debt.

We don't know the results of this, but they are unlikely to be good. The US debt might not be as worthless as Confederate bonds were in 1866. But they will be a lot less sterling than they were in 2000, when Bill Clinton had us on a path to long-term fiscal strength.

So What Would Ben Stein Do about this?

I would raise taxes. Now make no mistake; your servant hates to pay taxes. It pains me to write out those quarterly checks. I can't bear to see that money for which I have worked so hard over the years and decades disappear into the coffers of Uncle Sam.

I worked for that money. It's mine.

Only, by law, it *isn't* mine. According to the law, the government can take as much of it as they want. And if the law does not change to allow the government to take more of my hard-earned money, my country will be in dire financial straits. I do not want that to happen. My son and his wife just had a baby as I write this. I do not want my son and his bride and my granddaughter to live in an America that is a fiscal shambles. I know that rich people and well-to-do people can afford to pay more taxes. We simply have to do it, as unpleasant as that will be.

Yes, we should cut spending as much as we reasonably can. Yes, Medicare in particular should be cut. There are too many tests and too much looting of the system by doctors, labs, and hospitals. But in a world as dangerous as ours; where many other countries throughout the world hate us; and where two of the most dangerous, vicious nations on this earth—North Korea and Iran—either have or are about to have nuclear weapons; we do not want to cut defense by any but token amounts, if that.

Most of our nation's budget is made up of *untouchable* items like Social Security, interest on the national debt, pensions to federal and defense personnel, and Medicare. These can be cut, as mentioned above, but only in small measure.

The deficits are in very large measure. And there is just no way to eliminate them except to raise taxes. To say we can do it any other way is to dwell in a fantasy world.

I am sorry to say this, because I genuinely loved Mr. Bush—and still do—and Arthur Laffer has never been anything but friendly to me. But we got into this mess by lowering taxes. And we are going to have to get out of it by raising them. There is simply no other way. No Republican candidate for any high office will tell you that; but I just did. Of course, I am not a candidate for office and I stole that cute rhetorical trick from a speech by Walter Mondale long ago.

On the other hand, Keynesian deficit spending—short of spending as much as one spends on a world war—doesn't work either. That's the Democrats' Kool-Aid.

Meanwhile—somehow, some way—Guatemalan immigrants who don't speak English find jobs in an economy with unemployment above nine percent, while graduates of prestigious colleges don't find jobs.

Motivation is everything. Work discipline is everything.

For example . . . there is almost no unemployment in Utah. Why? They don't have oil. They don't have casino gambling. They have an incredibly well-motivated, disciplined, eager work force. That's what you learn in The Church of the Latter-Day Saints. That's what all Americans once knew. That's how we got to be number one: hard work and discipline.

Yesterday I went into a drugstore in West Los Angeles. The cashier kept a line of customers waiting while she sampled designer cupcakes her son had brought her—then took them around to the other cashiers . . . while we waited. That would not happen in Utah.

Obviously, if there were a real Depression, with a total failure of demand, we would have even disciplined and hardworking people out of work. But in today's America, there are plenty of jobs. It is simply that native-born Americans generally won't take the ones at the bottom of the ladder, and we as taxpayers pay them to stay home and play Solitaire on their computers.

If we stopped paying these people to simply sit around their homes, they might be as eager to work as the immigrants from Guatemala—and we might have a lot less unemployment. We do not need more tax cuts with a government that's already broke. We don't need more government stimulus. We need a work force that's willing and eager to work. That's how we'll get back to high prosperity—or won't.

I know this is heresy. But that's why you bought the book.

33

Benjyrama

OKAY, NOW AS the Beatles said in "Sgt. Pepper's Lonely Hearts Club Band," we're getting very near the end.

I'd like to tell you about who I am, just because it may tell you something about who you are.

My wife, a true saint, calls me *Benjyrama*. This name comes from a nickname that our old pal, Mopsy Strange Kennedy, called me back in law school days. She used to call me *Benjorama*, which was a takeoff on a movie screening technique of long ago called Cinerama. In Cinerama shows, an immense image would be projected upon three separate screens in a theater, surrounding the audience in a movie image that swallowed them up and engulfed them in the variety and spectacle of what was going on onscreen.

Around the World in 80 Days was a good example of Cinerama. A similar technique was used in *How the West Was Won*. If you ever have chance to see them in Cinerama, don't miss it.

Mopsy Kennedy thought I was a *Rama-like* animal. I was always doing a million different things and putting on a show in all of them.

My wife and I hardly ever get to see Mopsy any more. She's in Cambridge, Massachusetts, with the Van Snoots. But my wife is my constant companion. To her, I am still the whirling images of light and dark, stereophonic sound *Rama*.

I do a number of different things. I am an essayist, a commentator on every manner of subject on TV, a pitchman for various products and services, an economist, an actor, a comedian, a property owner, a lawyer, a teacher, a husband, a father, a grandfather, a dog fancier, and a swimmer in the warm, large pool at our home.

By and large, I am a happy guy. When my health is good, when I am working, when I am getting applause and laughter, I am content.

197

There are a few things I absolutely hate: long security lines at airports; burned, tasteless food, hotel rooms that smell of carpet cleaner and air *freshener* (really more like air poisoner); people who tell me they know they have seen me on TV but cannot remember my name, then ask me my name; self-made wedding vows that go on and on; six-cylinder cars that promise they have the kick of a V8 engine and never do; running out of orange juice; and *friends* who *need* to borrow money and never, and I mean, *never*, repay it.

I also loathe any kind of criticism directed at the United States of America from abroad. I feel that the United States. has been so good to the rest of the world that they should be doing constant hosannas of praise to us.

I really cannot stand racism in any form at all. I spent a good part of my youth organizing and struggling against racism, and I still feel rage when I encounter it.

Recently, a very close friend put me up for membership in an exclusive club in Indian Wells, California. I was blackballed because I am a Jew. I did not like that. I'll be honest: I hated that. On the other hand, in a free society, men and women in a private club should have the right to be around those they wish to be around.

The real problem is that the taxpayers are subsidizing that racism by allowing the club in question to have property-tax-free status as a nonprofit. I am not sure that our local schools should have been deprived of the revenue a property tax on that immense golf course and clubhouse would have been provided when that entity is violating the explicit policy of the state of California by explicitly having a racist membership policy.

If it's that important to the club to have only Gentile members, possibly they could pony up to pay tax on their spectacular course and clubhouse. However, it's a small thing. I can—and will—live and die without being a member of that club. But I cannot be still when human beings in this country are deprived of the right to vote because of their race. As

Robert Kennedy aptly said, once they get the right to vote, all other problems get solved. The ballot franchise is power. You may not be ever able to erase racism from the human heart. But the ballot can get it out of law. I think I'll have a talk with the people in Riverside County about that club. Maybe not, though. Live and let live.

Other things I dislike:

People who come up to me at airports and have long, rambling philosophical discourses to deliver. I simply don't want to hear them. I love meeting new people, but I have already heard as much philosophy as I need to hear. Most of it comes from persons who prefer to remain anonymous, and they have taught me enough.

I dislike many habits about myself; I eat way too much. I spend way too much. I am extremely weak about resisting other people's entreaties for help even though they often inconvenience me. I am the absolutely sloppiest person in the world with my papers. Getting my data in order to do my income tax is a staggeringly difficult, unpleasant process for me and anyone helping me.

Some things I love are lying in bed in a sunny room, with my dogs; reading prayers with my wife; and swimming in my nice, warm pool. The best of all is swimming in the pool at our home in Rancho Mirage, California: doing the backstroke and seeing a jet plane lit up at night come right over my head on the approach into Palm Springs International Airport. That experience has everything going for it: warmth, exercise, motion, and the airplane symbolizing freedom and power. My earliest memories are of watching airplanes high in the sky over Washington, DC. Even then, they spoke of freedom and escape. They still do. To be in that pool and feel the vibration of the jet as I do my laps, to see the aluminum and lights and contrails, sometimes to see them silhouetted against the moon, through the palm fronds—that is paradise to me.

I am grateful. I am in motion. I am Winged Mercury, as my wife used to call me, only with her southern accent, she pronounced it *Mer-curry*. And my wife is asleep nearby, and the dogs are waiting for me, and I am happy.

What do I want to do next? Keep on swimming, keep on whirling, keep on being grateful for my wife and my son and daughter-in-law and my sister.

I sometimes think I could write an entire book just on the aphorisms my sister has told me. Two of the best are, "Your basic human is not such a hot item," and "For women, it's about their looks. For men, it's about how much money they have." She's down-to-earth. I'm the dreamer.

If I am having a good day, it's Gratitude-O-Rama.

Index